SHORTER TREKS IN THE PYRENEES

About the Author

Since taking early retirement from his career as a physics and sports teacher, Brian Johnson has found time for three through-hikes of the Pacific Crest Trail, a 2700-mile round-Britain walk, 10 hikes across the Pyrenees from the Atlantic to the Mediterranean, a hike along the Via de la Plata from Seville to Santiago and a single summer compleation of the Munros (Scotland's 3000ft mountains), as well as climbing all the Scottish 2000ft-plus mountains. He has also completed a 2200-mile cycle tour of Spain and France and done multi-week canoe tours in Sweden, France, Spain and Portugal. In his younger days, Brian's main sport was orienteering, competing as well as coaching Bishop Wordsworth's School and South-West Junior Orienteering Squads. After retiring due to injury 25 years ago, he has now been able to return to orienteering, winning the British Middle Distance Championships for his age group in 2017 and a five-day international event in France in 2018.

He has walked and climbed extensively in summer and winter conditions in Britain, the Alps, the Pyrenees and California, often leading school groups. As a fanatical sportsman and games player, Brian competed to a high level in cricket, hockey, bridge and chess – his major achievement being to win the 1995/96 World Amateur Chess Championships.

Other Cicerone guides by the author

The GR10 Trail: Through the French Pyrenees
The GR11 Trail: The Traverse of the Spanish Pyrenees
The Pacific Crest Trail
Walking the Corbetts Volume 1: South of the Great Glen
Walking the Corbetts Volume 2: North of the Great Glen

SHORTER TREKS IN THE PYRENEES

7 GREAT ONE AND TWO WEEK CIRCULAR TREKS

by Brian Johnson

JUNIPER HOUSE, MURLEY MOSS,
OXENHOLME ROAD, KENDAL, CUMBRIA LA9 7RL
www.cicerone.co.uk

© Brian Johnson 2019
First edition 2019
ISBN: 978 1 85284 930 6

Printed in China on behalf of Latitude Press Ltd
A catalogue record for this book is available from the British Library.

Route mapping by Lovell Johns www.lovelljohns.com
All photographs are by the author unless otherwise stated.
Contains OpenStreetMap.org data © OpenStreetMap
contributors, CC-BY-SA. NASA relief data courtesy of ESRI

The routes of the GR®, PR® and GRP® paths in this
guide have been reproduced with the permission of the
Fédération Française de la Randonnée Pédestre holder of
the exclusive rights of the routes. The names GR®, PR® and GRP® are registered
trademarks. © FFRP 2019 for all GR®, PR® and GRP® paths appearing in this
work.

Front cover: Evening view of Pic du Midi d'Ossau, looking over Lac Gentau from
Refuge d'Ayous (Route 2, Stages 7 and 8)

CONTENTS

SUMMARY OF THE TREKS

Route no	Start/finish	Distance	Total ascent	Time	Page
Route 1	St-Jean-Pied-de-Port	194km	8100m	9 stages (52hr)	33
Route 2	Etsaut	141km	7900m	8 stages (42hr)	78
Route 3	Cauterets	186km	10,600m	11 stages (64hr)	108
Route 4	Barèges	70km	3900m	4 stages (21hr)	151
Route 5	Refugi dera Restanca	89km	4700m	7 stages (32hr)	169
Route 6	Ax-les-Thermes	125km	6500m	8 stages (41hr)	196
Route 7	Eyne	224km	11,000m	12 stages (65hr)	224

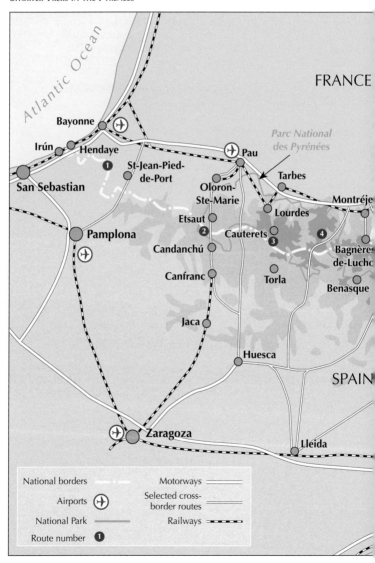

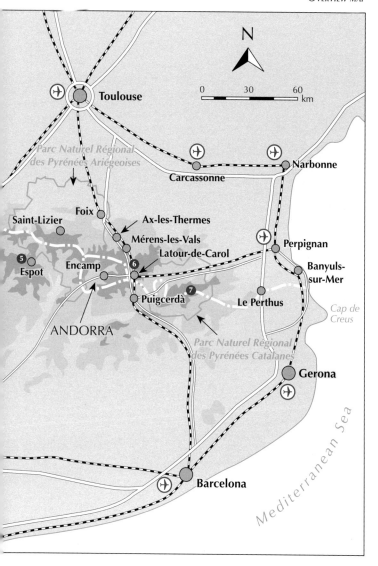

Mountain safety

Every mountain walk has its dangers, and those described in this guidebook are no exception. All who walk or climb in the mountains should recognise this and take responsibility for themselves and their companions along the way. The author and publisher have made every effort to ensure that the information contained in this guide was correct when it went to press, but, except for any liability that cannot be excluded by law, they cannot accept responsibility for any loss, injury or inconvenience sustained by any person using this book.

International distress signal *(emergency only)*
Six blasts on a whistle (and flashes with a torch after dark) spaced evenly for one minute, followed by a minute's pause. Repeat until an answer is received. The response is three signals per minute followed by a minute's pause.

Helicopter rescue
The following signals are used to communicate with a helicopter:

Help needed:
raise both arms
above head to
form a 'Y'

Help not needed:
raise one arm
above head, extend
other arm downward

Emergency telephone numbers
If telephoning from the UK the dialling codes are:
France: 0033
Spain: 0034

France: PGHM (Peloton de Gendarmerie de Haute Montagne):
tel 04 50 53 16 89; Emergency services: tel 112
Spain: Guardia Civil (responsible for mountain rescue): tel 112

Weather reports
France: www.meteo.fr or tel 3250
Spain: www.spainweather.es

Mountain rescue can be very expensive – be adequately insured.

Symbols used on route maps

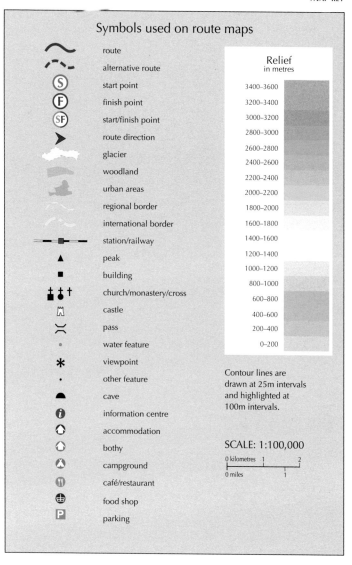

~ route

~ alternative route

(S) start point

(F) finish point

(SF) start/finish point

➤ route direction

glacier

woodland

urban areas

regional border

international border

station/railway

▲ peak

■ building

‡ church/monastery/cross

castle

✕ pass

· water feature

✱ viewpoint

· other feature

cave

ℹ information centre

accommodation

bothy

campground

café/restaurant

food shop

P parking

Relief
in metres

3400–3600	
3200–3400	
3000–3200	
2800–3000	
2600–2800	
2400–2600	
2200–2400	
2000–2200	
1800–2000	
1600–1800	
1400–1600	
1200–1400	
1000–1200	
800–1000	
600–800	
400–600	
200–400	
0–200	

Contour lines are drawn at 25m intervals and highlighted at 100m intervals.

SCALE: 1:100,000

0 kilometres 1   2

0 miles   1

The north face of Vignemale from Refuge des Oulettes de Gaube (Route 3, Stages 1 and 2)

PREFACE

I first discovered the Pyrenees about 40 years ago when I hiked the Pyrenean high-level route (Haute Route Pyrénées, or HRP) from Atlantic to Mediterranean over four summers. Since then I have completed 10 hikes from Atlantic to Mediterranean on the HRP, GR10 and GR11 and written the Cicerone guides to the GR10 and GR11. These are fantastic expeditions and are the ideal way to explore this magnificent mountain range, but most walkers cannot spare the time to be away from home for the 35–50 days most people take to complete these expeditions. Kev Reynolds has written an encyclopaedic guide for Cicerone on day-walking and climbing the major peaks in the Pyrenees, but there is no guide to shorter hut-to-hut or backpacking treks. This book is intended to fill the gap, with seven routes taking from four days to two weeks. I hope this will encourage you to take short treks in the Pyrenees and plan your own as well, using these as a base.

Except for the Carros de Foc, which is a promoted tour, the routes have been devised by the author to take you through the most spectacular parts of the Pyrenees and all have been walked at least twice in preparation of this guide.

The routes are designed so that it is possible to stay in accommodation each night, with meals and bed provided. Having said that, they are all magnificent routes for those walkers who prefer wild-camping to using huts and hotels. Use is made of the GR10, GR11, HRP, Camino de Santiago as well as less well-known long-distance and local paths.

Brian Johnson

GR10 hiker on Crête des Isards (Route 6, Stage 8)

INTRODUCTION

Achar d'Alano in the Sierra d'Alano (Route 2, Stage 3)

The Pyrenees is the diverse mountain chain which forms the border between France and Spain and stretches over 400km from the Atlantic Ocean to the Mediterranean Sea. The chain consists predominantly of granite massifs with rocky peaks dotted with lakes, tarns, cascading streams and spectacular waterfalls, and limestone mountains with vertical cliffs and the associated karst terrain.

Rising to over 3000m, the scenery compares favourably with the Alps, but the lower altitude means the highest peaks and passes are far more accessible to the hillwalker and backpacker. Although the treks in this guide are designed for those wanting overnight accommodation, with meals provided, the Pyrenees are almost certainly the best area in Europe for those who prefer wild-camping; it is still possible to find solitude and wilderness areas seemingly untouched by man. The predominantly dry, sunny summer climate is almost perfect for the backpacker, as is the relative absence of biting insects. It isn't just walkers who are attracted to the Pyrenees, however; it is a Mecca for birdwatchers, and for lovers of wildflower meadows and their associated butterflies.

The Pyrenees are also an interesting area culturally. While you may think of them as the border between France and Spain, there is also the enclave of Andorra, and much more significantly, the ancient nations of the Basque Country and Catalonia with their own languages and cultures.

For those who want a long trek it is suggested that you hike the GR10 or GR11, the coast-to-coast routes through France and Spain respectively, taking about 35–50 days. This guide provides treks that walkers could hike in a one- or two-week holiday. The seven featured routes are circular so that a minimum of time is wasted with transport.

Most of the time you will be walking on good, well-waymarked footpaths, but these are alpine mountains and on some of the routes there will be boulderfields to cross and some sections where use of hands will be needed when crossing high passes. Route 3, in particular, is at the highest difficulty that the 'average walker' would contemplate with a heavy pack. The routes are designed to be walked when they are free of snow and only those who are competent in walking/climbing in snow and ice conditions should consider walking them before the winter snow has melted (see 'Weather and when to go', below). Several of the routes are designed so

that they can be done as one long trek or split into two shorter treks.

OVERVIEW OF THE TREKS

Route 1: Tour of the Basque Country (9 stages)

This route takes you over the steep rolling hills in the Basque Country (in both France and Spain) at the western end of the Pyrenees. The terrain has similarities with the Welsh mountains and Scottish Highlands, except there are better paths, more sheep and horses, natural woodland rather than conifer plantation, warmer rain, hotter sun, and cheaper wine (or whisky)!

Accommodation is mainly in Basque villages with steep climbs leading to long walks along easy grassy ridges. This is the only route in the guide that traverses the highest mountains in the region and the views of the green Basque countryside are magnificent. You will have frequent sightings of griffon vultures and other birds of prey such as red kite when walking these ridges.

Apart from the quality of the route, this trek has been selected because it can be walked in May and June when the High Pyrenees are likely to impassable because of snow.

Route 2: Pic du Midi d'Ossau and the limestone peaks of the western Pyrenees (3, 5 or 8 stages)

The dramatic Pic du Midi d'Ossau, in the French Parc National des

Pyrénées, is probably the most photographed mountain in the Pyrenees and features as the cover photo on many guidebooks to the area.

This route takes in the magnificent limestone scenery at the western end of the High Pyrenees by combining the popular Tour du Pic du Midi d'Ossau, in France, with the best sections of the quieter La Senda de Camille on the Spanish side of the border. A descent of the intriguing Chemin de la Mâture is included.

The route is in eight stages but can easily be split into two treks of three and five stages.

Route 3: Tour de Vignemale and La Alta Ruta de Los Perdidos (5, 7 or 11 stages)

This is the most demanding trek in the guide with 'easy scrambling' over steep passes which would be challenging in bad weather or before the snow has melted. It is unlikely that the route would be feasible for the 'ordinary walker' until mid July.

The magnificent trek through the alpine terrain around Vignemale and Monte Perdido includes six of the 'honeypots' of the Pyrenees; Cauterets, Vignemale, Gavarnie, Pineta, Ordesa and the Picos del Infierno.

Although the route is designed in 11 stages there is a great deal of flexibility as you pass several other refuges and it would be possible to stay several nights at some of the refuges to explore these magnificent mountains. This route could easily be split into two separate walks; the Tour of Vignemale (seven stages) and the Tour de Monte Perdido (five stages).

Vignemale from Petit Vignemale (Route 3, Stage 2)

Route 4: Réserve Naturelle de Néouvielle (4 stages)

The shortest trek in this guide takes you through the popular Réserve Naturelle de Néouvielle and the surrounding mountains in the French Parc National des Pyrénées. It visits many lakes and tarns in magnificent granite scenery and there is the opportunity to climb several peaks, including Pic du Midi de Bigorre and Pic de Bastan. The trek is based around the GR10 and one of its variations, the GR10C.

Route 5: Carros de Foc (5 to 9 stages)

The Carros de Foc is an understandably popular trek in the magnificent Parc Nacional d'Aigüestortes i Estany de Sant Maurici, in the Spanish part of Catalonia. This is another granite massif dotted with hundreds of lakes and tarns. The route started as a challenge race visiting the nine refuges in the area in 24 hours but has become a well-walked hut-to-hut route. The huts are close together so there is a great deal of flexibility in planning, with most walkers taking 5–7 days for the trek.

Route 6: Tour des Montagnes d'Ax and the Tour des Péris (4, 6 or 8 stages)

The Ariège is a relatively unknown area at the eastern end of the High Pyrenees. This tour combines the magnificent alpine mountains of the Tour des Montagnes d'Ax on either flank of the Vallée de l'Ariège with the Tour des Péris in the gentler scenic mountains of the Cerdagne in the French part of Catalonia. This route is designed in eight stages, but suggestions are made for three alternative shorter tours.

Route 7: The icons of Catalonia: Puigmal and Canigou (5, 8 or 12 stages)

Our final tour goes through both the Spanish and French parts of Catalonia at the eastern end of the Pyrenees, taking in ascents of the two most climbed peaks in the Pyrenees; Puigmal and Canigou. Despite rising to almost 3000m the mountain ridges are gentler than in the High Pyrenees, more reminiscent of the Scottish Highlands, although the valleys still have an alpine feel. Much of the time is spent on spectacular high-level traverses of steep mountain slopes. This trek is likely to be free of significant snow by May or early June and is a good route for June or September. It would be easy to split this 12-stage trek into two shorter tours.

WEATHER AND WHEN TO GO

The prevailing wind in the Pyrenees is from the northwest which tends to mean that there is more cloud and rain in the north and west. The Spanish south-facing slopes are generally sunnier and drier than the north-facing French slopes and it is not unusual to have cloud in the French valleys while it is sunny above 2000m and in the Spanish valleys. The hills of the Basque Country have a reputation for mist and spells of gentle rain, but it is not unknown for temperatures to approach 40°C. The weather in the central Pyrenees is often hot and dry, but these are high mountains and can be subject to terrific thunderstorms. Thunderstorms in high mountains are usually thought of as being afternoon phenomena, but in the Pyrenees the storms are often slow to build up and can arrive in the evening or even in the middle of the night. As the Mediterranean is approached you are reaching a dry, arid region and can expect hot sunny weather.

Summer snowfall is unusual, but you could experience snow as low as 1500m in every summer month. There will be winter snow on the high passes well into summer, but this varies tremendously from year to year. In 2012 and 2017 the passes of the High Pyrenees were largely clear of snow by late June, but in 2013 there was still significant snow well into August.

The best months to walk the High Pyrenees are July, August and September, but if you are intending to walk Routes 1 or 7, you may prefer May, June or October when the weather will be cooler.

The main French and Spanish holiday season is from mid July to late August and booking accommodation will be essential during this period. Apart from at a few 'honeypot' areas, the mountains will be relatively quiet outside this period.

WILDLIFE

The Pyrenees, a Mecca for the bird-watcher, forms a big barrier to migrating birds which, in the spring and autumn, are funnelled along the

(L) Griffon vultures taking off from Pic d'Iparla; (R) alpine chough

Atlantic and Mediterranean coast-lines and through the lower passes. The casual birdwatcher will be most impressed with the large number of birds of prey.

The massive griffon vulture, with a wingspan of about 2.5m, will frequently be seen soaring on the high ridges, while the smaller Egyptian vulture, which is distinctively col-oured with a white body and black-and-white wings, is also likely to be seen. You may also see Europe's largest and rarest vulture, the lammergeier, which has a wingspan of up to 2.8m. The lammergeier feeds mainly on bone marrow which it gets at by dropping bones from a great height to smash them on the rocks below. Golden, booted, short-toed and Bonelli's eagles may also be seen. Arguably, the most beautiful bird you will see is the red kite with its deeply forked tail. You can also expect to see black kites, buzzards and honey buzzards as well as smaller birds of prey such as the kestrel, peregrine falcon, sparrowhawk and rarer birds such as the goshawk and even a migrating osprey.

One species that is thriving is the alpine chough, which you will see in large flocks. This member of the crow family is all black except for a yellow bill and red legs. Rarer small birds to look out for are the wallcreeper, crossbill, crested tit, red-backed shrike, bullfinch and alpine accentor.

You are much less likely to see some of the rare mammals that used to frequent the Pyrenees; brown bears have been reintroduced into the Ariège and are now spread over 9000km^2, but you are unlikely to see them, and the Pyrenean ibex was reintroduced in 2014 and there were about 100 in 2018. It is possible, but unlikely, that you will see wild boar and the reintroduced mouflon. You should have frequent sightings of the chamois (isard/izard), which was hunted to near extinction but has now made a remarkable recovery and increased to over 25,000. Other mammals you will see include marmots, several species of deer, foxes and red squirrels.

The most notable of these are the marmots, which are large ground squirrels that live in burrows. You will certainly know when they are present when you hear their alarm signal – a loud whistle, which sends them scurrying back into their burrows.

You are likely to see many reptiles and amphibians including the several species of snake, lizard, toad, frog and the dramatic fire salamander.

Unfortunately, the density of cattle, sheep and goats on the French side of the Pyrenees is high. You will often see *patou* (Pyrenean mountain dogs) guarding flocks of sheep. This large white dog has been used for hundreds of years by shepherds and you will often see unaccompanied flocks of sheep wandering the mountains guarded by these sheep-dogs. *Patou* are generally well trained and won't normally be aggressive as long

Patou sheepdog guarding its flock at Cabane d'Udapet (Route 2, Stage 1)

as you stay calm and steer clear of the flocks.

The Pyrenean flora is very diverse with at least 160 species of flower endemic to the Pyrenees as well as many species, such as edelweiss, that will be familiar to those who have visited the Alps. Wildflower meadows, which are home to a wide range of butterflies, are particularly spectacular in the wetter north-facing valleys of the French Pyrenees.

ACCESS

Access to the Pyrenees will be by plane, car, coach or train. Access information for each route is provided in the relevant route introduction, and useful websites are given in Appendix B.

By air

Barcelona and Toulouse are the most important airports for access to the Pyrenees but there are many local airports with connecting flights from Paris or Madrid. For UK readers, at the time of writing, Ryanair fly from Stansted and some regional airports to Biarritz, Lourdes, Carcassonne, Perpignan, Gerona and Barcelona. British Airways fly direct to Toulouse and Barcelona. Air France have flights from London to Pau and a big choice of destinations if you fly via Paris.

Clockwise from top left: large blue (butterfly); hedge bindweed; white asphodel; anemone narcissiflora; high brown fritillary (butterfly); edelweiss; martagon lily; spiny bear's breech

Easyjet fly from London to Biarritz and Bristol or London to Toulouse.

By car or coach

An alternative to driving down through France would be to take the car ferry to Bilbao or Santander (from Portsmouth or Plymouth with Brittany Ferries) in northern Spain. It is then an 80-mile drive from Bilbao or 130 miles from Santander to the western end of the Pyrenees. It is also possible to reach the Pyrenees by overnight coach from London (Victoria Coach Station): National Express run links to London and then FlixBus run coaches throughout Europe. The most convenient destinations are Irún and Figueras in Spain or Bayonne, Orthez, Pau, Tarbes, San-Gaudens, Toulouse and Perpignan in France.

By train and bus

Paris can be reached by Eurostar, from where SNCF run high-speed trains to a variety of destinations including Hendaye, Pau, Lourdes, Tarbes, Toulouse and Perpignan, from where there are rail and bus links to most main destinations in the Pyrenees. Likewise, there are bus and train routes from Barcelona to many convenient destinations in the Spanish Pyrenees.

ACCOMMODATION

Hotels in the Pyrenees vary greatly in quality and cost, but they will have all the facilities you would expect of a hotel in Britain. An **auberge** in France is the equivalent of an English inn. **Pensions** in Spain are rather like the British guest house.

Hostals in Spain are basic hotels; some will just offer accommodation, but most will also have a bar-restaurant. Note that a *hostal* is a cheap (minimum facility) hotel, not to be confused with a hostel (eg youth hostel in the UK, gîte d'étape in France or alberge in Spain).

Chambres d'hôtes in France and a **casa rural** or **turisme rural** in Spain are private houses offering accommodation similar to the British bed & breakfast (B&B). Many of them depend on weekly or weekend bookings and are reluctant to take advance bookings for a single night.

Gîtes d'étape in France are a network of cheap accommodation aimed primarily at walkers. They often have dormitory accommodation, but many also have smaller rooms. The more basic gîtes d'étape may only provide blankets but not bed linen. Most, but not all, will offer evening meals, breakfast and picnic lunches. Don't get confused by the 'gîte' designation; gîtes are mainly chambres d'hôtes rather than gîtes d'étape.

Albergues in Spain are 'youth hostels', but as in Britain most also take adults.

23

Manned refuges, **refugios or refugi** are mountain huts that offer accommodation, often in communal dormitories. They have a drink and meals service, open to both residents and non-residents, and most provide packed lunches.

Many **campgrounds**, especially those in Spain, will have cabins, normally called 'bungalows', and some will have bunkhouse accommodation.

Unmanned refugios, refugi, refuges or cabanes are open for the use of mountaineers and walkers. They are equivalent to the Scottish bothy. Some, particularly those in Andorra and Catalonia, are purpose-built and well-maintained. In France and Spain many of the 'bothies' are herdsmen's cabins which are no longer used by the herdsmen or are available when not occupied by them. Note that in many of the bothies the sleeping platform is hidden away in the roof-space. Some of the refuges marked on the maps are now ruins or little better than cow sheds.

If desperate for a place to stay, ask at the nearest bar-restaurant; they will often know locals who are willing to offer accommodation outside the official system.

Manned refuges

Manned refuges provide basic accommodation for walkers and climbers. They vary greatly in terms of the facilities and services provided, but a dormitory, bathroom and meals service are a minimum. Most people tend to book demi-pension (supper, bed and breakfast), and most refuges supply picnic lunches. Supper will normally be at 7pm or 7.30pm. Some refuges, but not all, have self-catering facilities.

Mattresses, blankets and pillows are provided in the dormitories, but a sleeping bag liner will be very useful. In most cases a 'camping' quality sleeping bag will be too warm for summer use. Although some refuges have private bedrooms, there is not normally segregation of the sexes in dormitories. Refuge hours and rules are designed for walkers, and therefore early 'lights out' at night as well as an early start in the morning should be expected.

Some refuges are open all year and others only during the summer; in the spring or autumn some will only be open at weekends but may open out of season if you make a reservation. In high summer and at weekends, booking ahead is strongly recommended.

Refuges offer a bar and snack service to walkers outside of normal mealtimes, and will normally have a room that can be used as a bothy when the refuge is closed. Camping is not permitted in the vicinity of many manned refuges; others will have a designated area for use by backpackers.

Many of the refuges don't have their own website but use a regional website which operates central booking (see Appendix B). Bear in mind that you may be able to get a discount if you are a member of an Alpine Association.

EQUIPMENT

Equipment is a matter of personal preference, but a few general points are made here:

- Keep your load as light as possible. If you don't need it, don't carry it!
- Even if you are using accommodation you will still want to carry a sheet sleeping bag and may decide to carry a lightweight sleeping bag and camping mat to enable you to bivouac if necessary

- Your waterproofs should be able to cope with thunderstorms in the High Pyrenees or steady rain in the Basque Country
- You should have sufficient clothing to cope with sub-zero temperatures
- A sun hat is strongly recommended
- Use plenty of sunscreen
- Shorts may be preferable to trousers, depending on the location and time of year in which you're hiking
- Good-quality walking shoes (approach shoes) are the best footwear. You could use lightweight boots, but heavy boots aren't necessary. Trainers aren't really robust enough for the terrain.

Refugio de Lizara (Route 2, Stages 4 and 5)

Make sure you have a good tread on your shoes or boots.

- As a minimum, if camping, you should have containers capable of carrying 3 litres of water, possibly with one easily accessible water bottle and the remaining capacity as water bags. If you are using huts you should still have a 2-litre capacity.

- It is strongly recommended that you use two walking poles to aid climbing, protect the knees on steep descents, to provide stability when crossing rough terrain, snowfields or mountain streams and for protection from dogs. If you are not carrying walking poles you may need an ice-axe to cope with snow on the high

passes. Crampons may be needed in early season in a high snow year.

CAMPING

In this guidebook the American term 'campground' is used for commercial or organised campsites, to distinguish them for wilderness campsites.

There are different laws about wild-camping in different parts of the Pyrenees but it is safe to assume that backpackers are allowed to bivouac for one night, with or without a small tent, well away from roads and habitation. In some areas the rules are defined, such as in 'Parc Natural' in Catalonia where wild-camping is permitted between 8pm and 8am, or the

Camping at Lac Blanc (Route 4, Stage 4)

French national parks where you may only bivouac at least an hour's walk from the roadhead.

You should ask permission if you want to camp near villages, in a farmer's fields, or close to a refuge. There is rarely any problem camping high in the mountains, but discretion should be used when camping at lower levels. The stages given in this guide are intended for walkers using accommodation overnight. Those who are wild-camping will want to ignore these stages and camp well away from the towns, villages and refuges.

If you are accustomed to always camping beside water you will sometimes have difficulty in finding a suitable campsite, especially on Routes 1 and 7. If you are prepared to camp away from water, you have much more flexibility and you can often find campsites with spectacular views.

It is good advice to wild-camp as high as possible as it is legal and there is less chance of being disturbed. There are also fewer cows and better grass, and fewer mosquitos and biting insects. But most of all there is magnificent scenery.

WATER

Water can be a problem in hot weather. When walking in temperatures of 25–30°C, you will need at least ½ litre (1 pint) of water for each hour of walking plus about 2 litres for a 'dry' camp. This is only a guideline; the precise requirement will vary

considerably from person to person and will depend on the temperature.

Most towns, villages and hamlets in the Pyrenees have fountains with untreated spring water. The locals and most walkers will drink the water without further treatment. 'Eau non potable', or similar terms, are widely seen on fountains in villages; this generally means that the water has not been treated or tested by the authorities. The main reason for the sign is the avoidance of any claim for compensation, rather than saying anything about the quality of the water.

You will often find fountains or 'piped' water as you walk along the trail. It should be obvious whether this water comes from a spring or a surface stream. Spring water is usually of a high quality and can be drunk with confidence. You should be more cautious about surface streams, especially streams in areas that are well stocked with sheep or cattle.

SWIMMING

Swimming is mentioned frequently in this guide. Pyrenean lakes and streams tend to be distinctly chilly until after snowmelt is complete. They never get really warm but in good weather can reach 20°C, which is comfortable. Conditions vary greatly from year to year; a lake on the GR11 that provided comfortable swimming in mid July 2012 still had ice on it in late July 2013!

There has always been a tradition of skinny-dipping in the mountain lakes and streams. A swimming costume is not essential for the 'lightweight' backpacker and skinny-dipping seems to be totally accepted by other users of the mountains.

FUEL

The three types of camping gas most commonly available in the Pyrenean region are:

- the ones you pierce – in this guidebook they are called 'original' cylinders
- the 'easy-clic' resealable cylinders, which is the main resealable system used in Southern Europe
- screw-on resealable cylinders, such as those manufactured by Coleman and Primus, which are the most widely used in Britain, Northern Europe and the USA – in this guidebook they are referred to as 'Coleman-style' gas cylinders.

'Coleman-style' cylinders are becoming more readily available, but the locals mainly use the 'original' or 'easy-clic' cylinders and these still are more widely available. In Spain, liquid fuels are most likely to be available at the local *ferreteria* (ironmongers) – but make sure you know what you are buying.

Note that gas cylinders are prohibited on planes and on the Eurostar so will have to be bought locally.

Lac d'Aumar (Route 4, Stage 4)

CULTURE AND LANGUAGE

Spanish siesta
Even on the French side of the border, in the villages, you can expect shops to be open in the morning, closed during the afternoon and open again in the evening. In larger towns they are more likely to be open all day.

Languages
Although you may think you are walking through the French or Spanish Pyrenees, many locals won't think of themselves as French or Spanish.

In the Basque Country (including the north of Navarre) the main language is Euskera (Basque). Basque is also widely spoken in the French part of the Basque Country. In Andorra and (Spanish) Catalonia the main language is Catalan, but on the French side of Catalonia it will normally be French. It is less likely that you will encounter Aragonés and Aranés, but you will see the legacy of these languages in the confusion of place names. English is now spoken much more widely than it was in the 20th century, especially by younger people.

There is a lot of confusion with names in the Pyrenees, with many different names and spellings for the villages and geographical features. French and Spanish names were imposed by the centralised governments but with greater autonomy there is a reintroduction of Basque and Catalan names. New signposts are increasingly using Basque, Aragonés or Catalan names whereas the French or Spanish maps still often use the French or Spanish name.

Politics
When they were independent states, the Basque Country and Catalonia were much larger than at present and included large chunks of the Pyrenees that are now in France. They still have a great deal of autonomy and the independence movements in both provinces have a lot of support.

The Spanish Civil War had a devastating effect on the people of the Pyrenees and the effects can still be seen today with the destruction or desertion of many mountain villages. The civil war broke out in

The unofficial Catalan flag used by the independence movement

1936 with a coup d'état by right-wing elements in the army. The position in the Pyrenees was particularly complicated as there were not only the Fascist and Republican armies, but also independence movements among the Catalans and the Basques. By the time the Republicans were defeated in 1939 about 700,000 lives had been lost and about 500,000 refugees had fled across the Pyrenees into France.

Andorra

This guide doesn't include a route in Andorra as the best routes would require the use of unmanned refuges, but if you do visit Andorra you should be aware that it is not in the European Union, despite using the euro. This means that if you buy 'duty-free' products there, you have not paid tax in an EU country – and customs controls are often in operation on road crossings to France or Spain. Catalan is the official language, but English, French and Spanish are widely spoken.

USING THIS GUIDE

The daily stages in this guidebook have been organised with the walker who wants to use accommodation in mind. See Appendix A for route summary tables. Those who are camping

GR red/white waymarking

are advised to ignore these stages and to camp well away from towns and villages. Accommodation is limited at the endpoint of some stages so booking would be advisable in peak season.

In good visibility, when the ground is free of snow, it is possible to follow the routes using waymarking, the route description and the 1:100,000 maps in this guidebook. However, you should carry more detailed maps as you will need them in bad weather, when there are extensive snowfields, or if you leave the described route, whether deliberately or accidentally. The relevant sheet maps are listed in each route introduction. Features that appear on the maps in the book are shown in **bold** in the route text.

Most navigational mistakes occur because the walker does not look at the map or guidebook until they are lost. The route descriptions and maps in the guide are designed to prevent you getting lost and they will be of little use when you are lost. Keep your map and guidebook handy, not buried in your rucksack.

When you are following GR routes, such as the GR11 in Spain and GR10 in France, the routes will have excellent red/white waymarking. Waymarking of local paths and other long-distance paths tends to be less efficient, often using a similar system with yellow/white or yellow/green waymarks. In the high mountains waymarking can be sparser and supplemented by cairns.

Timings
The timings given in this guide are the actual walking times recorded by the author on a GPS device while backpacking the route. In theory, but not always in practice, the GPS should stop recording during short breaks and breathers and it probably slightly overestimates the time taken. Your own walking time will obviously depend on factors such as navigational ability, fitness, load, group size, conditions and whether you like long breaks, so you should adjust the timings accordingly – you may want to add as much as 50% to the guidebook time. Times to climb peaks assume you are walking without a pack. Timings are not given for side-routes that the author has not walked himself when researching this guide.

Distances, ascents and height profiles
Distances don't mean very much in the Pyrenees where the steepness or roughness of the terrain can be a lot more important than the distance or even the amount of ascent. Distances given in this guidebook have been recorded by a GPS device, which will probably slightly over-record the distance, so they may differ from signposts and other guidebooks which often significantly underestimate it. The ascent has been estimated from the maps and actual GPS readings. The height profiles are intended to show the general trend of the day's

Looking across Col d'Harrieta towards Astate (Routes 1 and 2)

walk and won't show all ups and downs.

GPX tracks

A GPS device is not needed to follow the routes, but GPS co-ordinates (latitude and longitude) have been included for key points along the route for those who prefer to use one.

A GPS device is an excellent aid to navigation, but you should also carry a map and compass and know how to use them.

ROUTE 1

Tour of
the Basque Country

Start/finish	St-Jean-Pied-de-Port
Distance	194km
Total ascent/descent	8100m
Time	9 stages (52hr)

This is a demanding high-level traverse of the mountains and steep rolling hills in the Basque Country at the west end of the Pyrenees. There are long, steep climbs from the villages that offer overnight accommodation and long walks along easy grassy ridges. The ridges are exposed, and you are likely to have to contend with sun or cloud and rain. This is the only route in this guide that traverses the highest mountains in the region and the views of the Basque countryside are spectacular.

Much of the route is on well-waymarked sections of the GR10, GR11 and Camino de Santiago, so navigation is generally straightforward. Griffon vultures are thriving in the Basque Country and you will have close views of these magnificent birds on all stages of route. You should see many other species of birds of prey, with the red kite also being a common sight.

There is no problem finding wild campsites, but you are advised to camp high, in the realm of sheep and horses, rather than in the valleys with cows and the rules of 'civilisation'. There are spectacular exposed wild campsites on the high ground throughout the route, but you should be prepared to carry water to a dry camp as the opportunity to camp beside water is limited. Resupplying along the route is easy as there are food shops throughout.

The route will normally be free of snow by April and it is best to visit the area in spring or autumn rather than in high summer when it could be very hot and accommodation tends to be fully booked by tourists – May or June are recommended.

Basque will be the main language on the Spanish side of the border with Spanish as a second language. Surprisingly, you will probably find English more useful than French. The locals on the French side of the border will speak either Basque or French as a first language, but you can expect everyone to speak French.

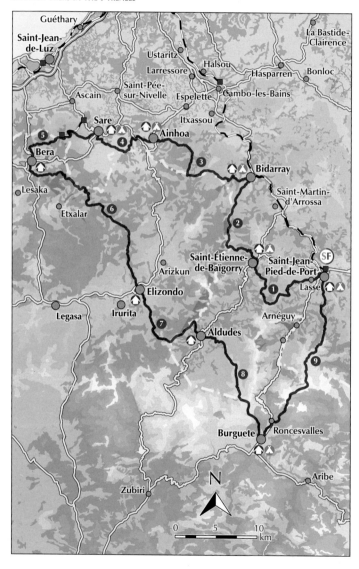

GR10 hikers in St-Jean-Pied-de-Port

Access

The route description starts at St-Jean-Pied-de-Port, which offers easy access by rail on the branch line from Bayonne. It is also possible to access Bidarray (Stage 3) on this line. From St-Jean-Pied-de-Port there are buses to Sare (Stage 5) and St-Étienne-de-Baïgorry (Stage 2). There is road access on every stage of the route, so you could begin your trek further along if you prefer.

Maps

- IGN Pyrénées Carte no 1, *Pays Basque Ouest* at 1:50,000 covers Stages 1–6
- IGN Pyrénées Carte no 2, *Pays Basque Est* at 1:50,000 covers Stages 1–2 and 9
- Editorial Alpina *GR11 map* at 1:50,000 covers Stages 6–8
- FFRandonnée Topoguides *La Traversée des Pyrénées: Pyrénées Occidentales* at 1:50,000 covers Stages 1–4

STAGE 1
*St-Jean-Pied-de-Port to
Saint-Étienne-de-Baïgorry*

Start	St-Jean-Pied-de-Port
Distance	20km
Total ascent	900m
Total descent	900m
Time	5hr 15min
High points	Munhoa (1021m)

St-Jean-Pied-de-Port is the most popular starting point for the Camino de Santiago, a network of pilgrim routes from all over Europe leading to the shrine of the apostle Saint James in the cathedral of Santiago de Compostela in northwest Spain, where tradition has it that the remains of the saint are buried. The town is a major tourist resort with tourist office, several campgrounds, a wide range of accommodation, bar-restaurants and shops to cater for both the tourist and Camino de Santiago 'pilgrim'. Maya Sport, which stocks walking equipment and all types of camping gas, is beside the Carrefour supermarket.

This easy first stage follows the GR10, with red/white waymarks, over Munhoa with the option of the ascent of Oylarandoy.

Start at the roundabout at the south end of **St-Jean-Pied-de-Port** (N43°09.791 W001°14.339) where there are toilets and a water point. Head northwest along the D933, forking right along the D918 and then left just before the Lidl supermarket to pick up the D403 towards Lasse. Follow the D403 right across a bridge and on to the Auberge Etchoinia in **Lasse** (**30min**). Opposite the auberge are public toilets with a water point and free hot showers.

Keep on past the church, then turn left and right and fork left. Pass a farm with a water point and ignore three right turns before reaching a track on the right, signed to

Route 1 – Stage 1 – St-Jean-Pied-de-Port to Saint-Étienne-de-Baïgorry

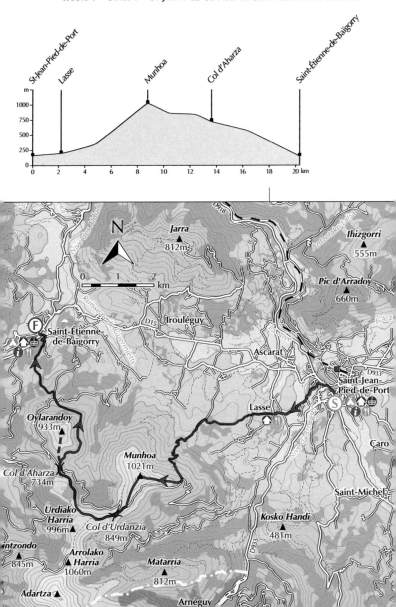

Munhoa (**1hr 5min**, 360m, N43°09.203 W001°17.233). Turn right and follow the track as it switchbacks up the hill to reach a farm road at a water point on the east ridge of Munhoa (**2hr 10min**, 745m). ◄ Cross the road and go diagonally right, soon recrossing the road and climbing the ridge to the mast on the summit of **Munhoa** (**2hr 55min**, 1021m, N43°08.521 W001°18.425).

In bad weather you have the option of following this road all the way to Saint-Etienne-de-Baïgorry.

Descend the southwest ridge, turning right on returning to the road. Go straight on at a junction on the **Col d'Urdanzia** and climb gently, passing below a barn before a path goes off right (**3hr 25min**, 920m, N43°07.899 W001°19.345). Follow this path which goes just below the Col de Leizarze and turn right on reaching a farm road. Follow this to the **Col d'Aharza**, with a water point by the sheepfolds (**4hr**, 734m, N43°08.689 W001°20.111).

If you have surplus energy you could climb the ridge to the north to the summit of **Oylarandoy** (933m) where a hermitage was first built in 1706. The shrine has been rebuilt on several occasions and the latest (1985) rebuild even includes stained-glass windows. You could then rejoin the GR10 down the steep bracken-covered northeast ridge, however it would be easier to leave your rucksack at the col and return down the south ridge (up and down in 35min).

From the Col d'Aharza, follow the GR10 which goes right of the pens and contours the eastern slopes of Oylarandoy, passing a barn with a water point before reaching the northeast ridge. Veer sharp left along a track, then right down a concrete track and straight on down the road before forking left down another track. Keep straight on down a path at a bend in the track and take the descending option at every junction until you turn left under the old railway bridge to arrive at the bridge over La Nive des Aldudes in **Saint-Étienne-de-Baïgorry** (**5hr 15min**, 158m, N43°10.642 W001°20.522).

Saint-Étienne-de-Baïgorry is a village with two supermarkets, a range of accommodation, bar-restaurants and shops. Most of the facilities are to the left, but the tourist office and pizzeria are to the right.

FACILITIES FOR STAGE 1

St-Jean-Pied-de-Port (a small selection of the available accommodation)

Tourist office: tel (33) 0559 37 03 57 www.saintjeanpieddeport-paysbasque-tourisme.com

Camping Municipal Plaza Berri: tel (33) 0559 37 11 19

Gîte d'étape Compostella: tel (33) 0559 37 02 36

Gîte d'étape Ultreïa: tel (33) 0680 88 46 22 www.ultreia64.fr

Hôtel Les Remparts: tel (33) 0559 37 13 79 www.hoteldesremparts.fr

Hôtel Central: tel (33) 0559 37 00 22

Lasse

Auberge Etchoinia has accommodation and bar-restaurant: tel (33) 0559 37 01 57 www.auberge-etchoinia-pays-basque.com

Saint-Étienne-de-Baïgorry

Tourist office: tel (33) 0559 37 47 28 www.pyrenees-basques.com

Gîte Gaineko Karrikan has chambres d'hôtes, gîte d'étape and meals: tel (33) 0559 37 47 04 or (33) 0625 19 18 67 http://gitospit.free.fr

Gîte d'étape Mendy is at the Domaine de Leispars about 1.5km northeast of Saint-Étienne-de-Baïgorry: tel (33) 0559 37 42 39

Villages VVF Iparla is mainly aimed at tourists but will take hikers: tel (33) 0559 37 40 58 www.vvf-villages.fr

Camping Municipal Irouleguy: tel (33) 0559 37 40 80

Hôtel-restaurant Arce: tel (33) 0559 37 40 14 www.hotel-arce.com

Hôtel-restaurant Juantorena: tel (33) 0559 37 40 78 www.hotelrestaurant juantorena.fr

STAGE 2
Saint-Étienne-de-Baïgorry to Bidarray

Start	Saint-Étienne-de-Baïgorry
Distance	19km
Total ascent	1400m
Total descent	1400m
Time	6hr 45min
High points	Buztanzelhay (1029m), Astate (1022m) and Pic d'Iparla (1044m)

This demanding stage follows the GR10 as it traverses the magnificent Pic d'Iparla ridge, arguably the most spectacular ridge in the Basque Country.

In **Saint-Étienne-de-Baïgorry**, cross the bridge over la Nive des Aldudes and follow the road right to a square

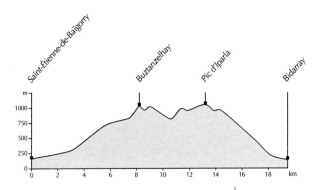

with tourist office, toilets, water point, bar-restaurant and pizzeria. Take the road at the far left corner of the square, go left at the Gendarmerie and past the VVF holiday centre. Shortcut right up a path after a cattle grid and, shortly after returning to the farm road, turn left up a path (**40min**, 300m, N43°11.310 W001°21.020) and climb steeply.

Eventually rejoin the farm road and soon pass a water point (**1hr 25min**), the last reliable water on the stage. Continue up the track, ignoring a couple of shortcuts on the left, to reach the roadhead at the **Col d'Apaloy** on the east ridge of Aintziaga (**1hr 50min**, 716m, N43°11.294 W001°22.267).

Follow the path along the left-hand side of the ridge to the next col (**2hr**). Cross the col and traverse the rough undulating path on the steep north slopes of Aintziaga to reach a small stream, which could dry up in a hot summer. Follow the stream up to the col, **Buztanzelaiko Lepoa** (**2hr 35min**, 843m, N43°11.469 W001°23.076). The ridge, which is rough and rocky in places, is now followed all the way to Bidarray. Care will be needed with navigation in mist.

Turn right; the path goes up the left-hand side of the ridge, to avoid crags, to arrive at the summit of **Buztanzelhay** (**3hr 5min**, 1029m, N43°11.661 W001°23.199). Descend to the **Col d'Astate** (957m) with

41

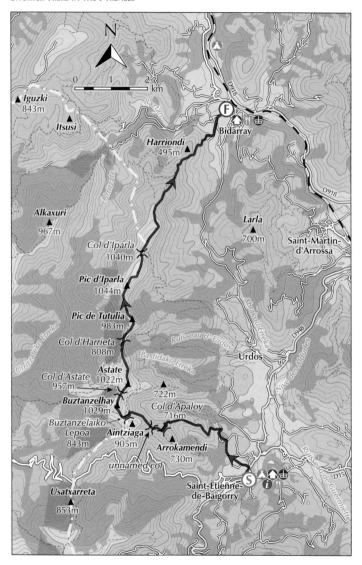

N

0 1 2 km

▲ *Iguzki*
843m

▲ *Itsusi*

Harriondi
495m

Bastan

(F)
Bidarray

D918

D918

Urritzate

Larla
700m

Saint-Martin-
d'Arrossa

▲ *Alkaxuri*
967m

Col d'Iparla
1040m

Pic d'Iparla
1044m

Abakroui Erreka

D948

Pic de Tutulia
983m

Ruisseau d' Urdos

Col d'Harrieta
808m

Bastidako Erreka

Urdos

Urritzaeko Erreka

Astate
1022m

Col d'Astate
957m →

▲
722m

Buztanzelhay
1029m

Col d'Apaloy
716m

*Buztanzelaiko
Lepoa*
843m

▲
Aintziaga
905m

Arrokamendi
730m

Nive des Aldudes

unnamed col

(S)
*Saint-Etienne-
de-Baigorry*

▲ *Usatxarreta*
853m

Ruisseau de Guermiette

D15

the remains of a dolmen (ancient burial chamber) and climb **Astate** (**3hr 25min**, 1022m). Descend gently, then more steeply through woods to the **Col d'Harrieta** (**3hr 55min**, 808m, N43°12.652 W001°23.057). ▶ A sign points to a water point 300 metres to the southwest, but it is of dubious quality and reliability.

There is an escape route east to Urdos which you could take in extreme weather.

Continue up **Pic de Tutulia** (**4hr 20min**, 983m, N43°12.927 W001°22.879) and descend a little before climbing the ridge to **Pic d'Iparla** with a trig point (**4hr 55min**, 1044m, N43°13.694 W001°22.701). Descend to borderstone 90 at the **Col d'Iparla** and follow the north-northeast ridge, possibly bypassing a couple of minor tops, before passing a possible water point where water is being fed into a pond (**5hr 30min**). About 8min later the GR10 descends slightly right and does a descending traverse of the east-facing slopes, to avoid crags, before returning to the ridge. A path joins from back left (**6hr**) and about 7min later (454m, N43°15.275 W001°21.805) descend right into the woods to reach a farm (**6hr 30min**).

Pic d'Iparla

Follow the farm road to the top of **Bidarray**. The GR10 goes left, but turn right for the facilities. The hotel is opposite the church which has water points and a toilet hidden in the churchyard (**6hr 45min**, 145m, N43°15.930 W001°20.893).

The main facilities in **Biderray** for walkers are in the upper village where there is a small shop in the bar-restaurant Iparla complex and the Hôtel Barberaenea. Bidarray is on the railway line between Bayonne and St-Jean-Pied-de-Port. The station and the Hôtel Noblia are in the lower village beside the river. Camping Amestoya is also on the D918, about 2km north of Bidarray.

FACILITIES FOR STAGE 2

Bidarray

Hôtel Barberaenea: tel (33) 0559 37 74 86 www.hotel-bidarray.com

Hôtel-restaurant Noblia: tel (33) 0559 37 70 89 www.hotel-basque-noblia.com

Camping Amestoya: tel (33) 0559 37 25 81 https://camping-bidarray.fr

Accommodation may be available at the Arteka adventure school, if not fully booked for courses: tel (33) 0559 37 71 34 www.arteka-eh.com

STAGE 3

Bidarray to Ainhoa

Start	Bidarray
Distance	26km
Total ascent	900m
Total descent	900m
Time	6hr 30min
High points	Col de Méhatché (716m), Gorospil (691m) and Erebi (583m)

The stage continues along the GR10, with rolling hills replacing the mountains but still with spectacular views.

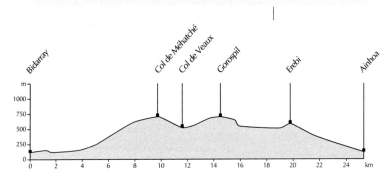

Return to the west end of **Bidarray** and keep straight on. Fork left up a road which soon becomes a track, ignore a left turn and a fork right before forking right and descending to a road. Turn left alongside **Le Bastan**, fork right and cross the bridge over the river (**50min**). After the fourth switchback in the road, switchback right up a path (**1hr 15min**, 250m, N43°15.802 W001°23.060).

> Ignore a side-path which goes steeply right to the **Grotte du Saint qui Sue** (Harpeko Saindua). Legend suggests that a young shepherdess was found 'petrified' in the rock. The cave became a shrine and site of pilgrimage with claims that the 'holy water' oozing through the rock would cure skin and eye diseases.

Soon pass the first obvious campsite since Bidarray (**1hr 35min**). ▶ There now follows an ascent of a steep rocky path with hand-lines to protect a few exposed sections, to arrive at a signpost on the ridge (**2hr 45min**, 640m, N43°16.025 W001°23.910). Head north-north-west along the ridge, passing borderstones 83 and 82

Keep an eye out for rock martins here.

45

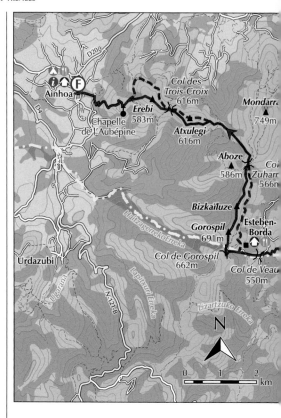

before arriving at a road col, **Col de Méhatché**, with the remains of a dolmen (**3hr 10min**, 716m, N43°16.378 W001°24.993).

> You could climb **Artzamendi** (926m) from here, following the tarmac road to the communications complex on the summit, or **Pic Iguzki** (844m) by its grassy northeast ridge.

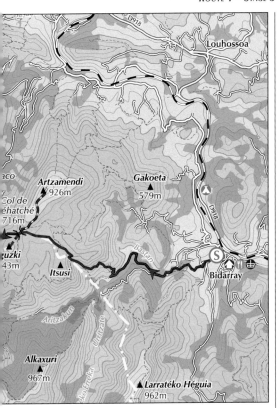

To continue on the main route from the col, turn left along the road then, when the road switchbacks right, keep straight on along a path and follow paths and tracks to the road col at **Col de Veaux** (535m). There is a sign to Venta Burkaitz with bar-restaurant and accommodation, in Spain, which is about 300 metres south of the Col des Veaux.

Continue straight on up to the front entrance to Esteben-Borda, a gîte d'étape with bar-restaurant. The GR10 forks left up a track, passing borderstone 77 to reach the back entrance to Esteben (**3hr 50min**, 560m, N43°16.067 W001°26.492).

The GR10 now turns right and traverses the east slopes of the Gorospil ridge, but that should be seen as the bad-weather option. Instead, keep straight on up the concrete track to the **Col de Gorospil** (662m) and turn right over **Gorospil** (691m) and along the hogsback ridge to the **Col de Zuharreteaco** (**4hr 45min**, 566m, N43°17.359 W001°26.312) with pipe-fed spring water (dry June 2018) and rejoin the GR10.

Descend diagonally left and follow a good track to a col (**5hr**) and a second col before starting a rising traverse of the south slopes of **Atxulegi** (it would be possible to traverse this peak) to arrive at the **Col des Trois-Croix** (**5hr 30min**, 513m, N43°18.157 W001°27.931) which has one small cross!

The GR10 veers right and traverses the northern slopes of Erebi, but in good weather you should keep straight on and climb **Erebi** (**5hr 45min**, 583m). The descent route isn't obvious; initially continue along

Crucifixion of Christ at the Chapelle de l'Aubépine

the northwest ridge then soon veer left and pick up a path down the broad west ridge, rejoining the GR10 just above the **Chapelle de l'Aubépine** with three large crosses depicting the crucifixion of Christ (**6hr**, 404m, N43°18.207 W001°28.932).

Follow the gravel road down, soon passing a water point and nine large crosses before following tarmac roads past toilets, a water point and the tourist office to arrive at the main street in **Ainhoa**, by the church (**6hr 30min**, 131m, N43°18.395 W001°29.929).

Ainhoa is a tourist village with three hotels and a campground with gîte d'étape. There are many small shops for the tourist but the only food available is bread, cheese and Basque specialities at tourist prices.

FACILITIES FOR STAGE 3

Col de Veaux

Venta Burkaitz has a bar-restaurant, gîte d'étape and camping is possible, but it is only open in high summer: tel (34) 0948 393 000 (Spanish) or (33) 0559 29 82 55 (French).

Ferme Esteben has a bar-restaurant and gîte d'étape: tel (33) 0559 29 82 72 www. gites-refuges.com/v2/detail-1868.htm

Ainhoa

Tourist office: tel (33) 0559 29 93 99 www.ainhoa.fr

Camping Harazpy also has a gîte d'étape. No meals: tel (33) 0559 29 89 38 www.camping-harazpy.com

Hôtel la Maison Oppoca: tel (33) 0559 29 90 72 www.oppoca.com

Hôtel Argi Eder: tel (33) 0559 93 72 00 www.argi-eder.com

Hôtel Ithurria: tel (33) 0559 29 92 11 www.ithurria.com

STAGE 4
Ainhoa to Sare

Start	Ainhoa
Distance	13km
Total ascent	200m
Total descent	200m
Time	2hr 55min

This stage is still following the GR10 but you need to keep a careful eye on the red/white waymarks as route-finding can be complex. A strong walker might consider combining Stages 4 and 5. This is the Basque Country and the many ups and downs in this undulating stage aren't obvious from the stage profile. The path can be very muddy when wet.

From the church head south down the main street in **Ainhoa**, going straight on at the end and following the waymarks carefully to pick up the road heading WSW out of the village. Fork right, then left down a path (**15min**) and fork right just before you reach the river. The path becomes a track which takes you left across the river, then turn right up the left bank. Cross a road (**45min**) and

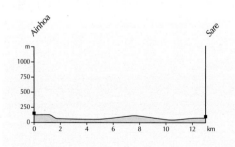

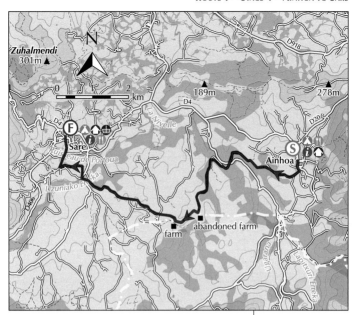

head down a dirt road before forking left along a track.
Cross the dirt road when you next meet it and head up a
tributary of the river. Rejoin the track and cross the river
(**1hr 5min**, 64m, N43°18.101 W001°31.833).

Eventually the track veers right by an **abandoned
farm** and follows the border for a bit before turning right
at a **farm** and continuing to a road junction (**1hr 50min**).
Keep straight on, ignoring a left turn, and follow the road
as it becomes a farm track. The main track soon turns left
(no waymarks in 2018), then turn right along a road. As
you descend towards the river keep a close eye on the
waymarks as you need to find an easily missed left turn
down a path to cross the river (**2hr 25min**).

Keep straight on if you want the Hôtel Pikassaria
or Camping la Petite Rhune, which has a gîte d'étape.
Otherwise, turn right along the main road and almost
immediately fork left up some cobbled steps. Pass a

Cobbled path in Sare

water point, turn left along a road at the end of the cobbled path and then sharp right down another cobbled path (**2hr 40min**). Keep straight on to the church square in the centre of **Sare** (**2hr 55min**, 78m, N43°18.675 W001°34.806).

> **Sare** is a small village with a tourist office, campground and many small shops. There is a bus service from Sare connecting with the rail network at St-Jean-de-Luz. You pass the Spar supermarket early in Stage 5.

FACILITIES FOR STAGE 4

Sare

Hôtel-restaurant Pikassaria: tel (33) 0559 54 21 51 www.hotel-pikassaria.com

Camping la Petite Rhune, also has a gîte d'étape. No meals but nearby bar-restaurant: tel (33) 0559 54 23 97 www.lapetiterhune.com

Tourist office: tel (33) 0559 54 20 14 www.sare.fr

Hôtel Arraya: tel (33) 0559 54 20 46 www.arraya.com

Hôtel-restaurant Lastiry: tel (33) 0559 54 20 07 www.hotel-lastiry.com

STAGE 5
Sare to Bera (Vera de Bidasoa)

Start	Sare
Distance	17km
Total ascent	900m
Total descent	900m
Time	4hr 50min
High points	La Rhune (905m)

La Rhune, a fabulous viewpoint on a clear day, has been prominent on the skyline for a couple of days and now the route climbs it and descends into Spain to join the GR11. The first section is still on the GR10 with red/white waymarking.

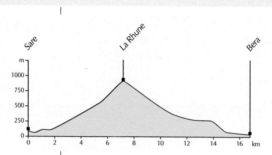

Go left past the church in **Sare**, then keep straight on, turn left and right to go between the *fronton* (a court for the Basque sport of *pelota*) and swimming pool. Here

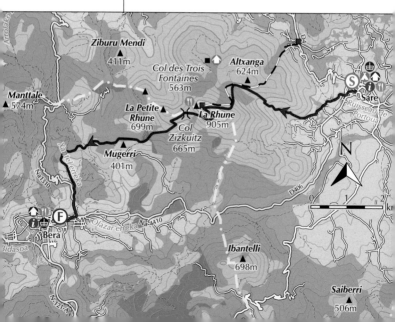

you will find toilets, water and the Spar supermarket. Go down steep path and turn left and right, cross the main road and veer right up a minor road. When this road goes sharp left, keep straight on along a path to reach a roadhead.

Follow the road, turning right at a junction and continue to another roadhead (**45min**, 175m, N43°18.352 W001°35.936). Continue along the track, ignoring many minor junctions, but forking left at two major junctions. Once above the main treeline turn right to cross the stream (**1hr 25min**, 360m) and then left to continue the climb to reach La Rhune **mountain railway** (**2hr**, 540m, N43°18.864 W001°37.445) at the east side of the broad and complex **Col des Trois Fontaines**. There are a several water sources on the col, but you will probably want to treat the water before drinking. There is a small bothy a short distance north of the west side of the col.

This is where you leave the GR10 and the route isn't waymarked. Don't cross the railway but instead climb roughly south up a path to a bend in the railway. Veer

La Rhune

right here, staying left of the railway, to reach the summit of **La Rhune** with railway station, communications masts, bar-restaurants and souvenir shops (**3hr**, 905m, N43°18.543 W001°38.136).

Follow the good track down the ESE ridge, switch-backing to reach **Col Zizkuitz** (**3hr 20min**, 665m) and borderstone 23 on the west ridge of La Rhune. Continue down the track to a junction on a col (**3hr 45min**, 360m) and fork right along the north slopes of **Mugerri** (401m). At the next col, a six-way junction (**4hr 5min**, 280m, N43°17.959 W001°40.491), take the track descending southwest, signed to Bera. Turn left down a concrete track (**4hr 15min**) and follow this down past houses to reach the stream and a water point and soon cross the stream. Turn left and follow the road into **Bera**, then right to the centre where there is a GR11 signboard in the main car park (**4hr 50min**, 40m, N43°16.836 W001°40.936).

> **Bera** is a small town with a tourist office (public toilets inside), a selection of accommodation and an excellent supermarket.

FACILITIES FOR STAGE 5

Bera tourist office: tel (34) 948 631 222

Hostal Auzoa: tel (34) 654 385

Hostal Zalain: tel (34) 948 630 967 https://zalain.info/hostal

Hotel Churrut: tel (34) 948 625 540 http://hotelchurrut.com

Casa Rural Romano: tel (34) 948 631 137

STAGE 6
Bera to Elizondo

Start	Bera
Distance	33km
Total ascent	1200m
Total descent	1000m
Time	8hr 20min
High points	Santa Barbara (384m), Col de Nabarlasta (477m), Collado Achuela (795m)

The route now follows the GR11 with good red/white waymarking over rolling hills. This is a long, but easy stage. It may be possible to split it into two stages if the new accommodation planned for 2019 at the Collado de Lizarrieta comes into being.

Head up the road right of the car park in **Bera**, passing the swimming pool and reaching a water point (**15min**). Fork right up a track, fork left twice, then right, returning to the concrete track. Follow a good track above the last house, turn sharp left onto open hillside and veer right to the summit of **Santa Barbara** with pill box, memorials and sculptures (**1hr 5min**, 384m, N43°15.957 W001°40.309).

Veer left along the edge of the wood and straight on at a col and over **Sorokogaña** (359m). At the end of the wood, climb the stile and cross the field, aiming to the right of the white house. Continue down the concrete drive and, at the bottom (**1hr 30min**, 270m), follow the track right and left. Fork right on a smaller track, turn left by a barn and fork right at the next barn before veering right (**1hr 55min**) to contour the southwest slopes of Ibanteli (Labeaga). Cross a small stream before arriving at the **Collado de Lizarrieta** and borderstone 44. Venta Lizaieta, the bar-restaurant, reopened under new management in 2018 with the intention of

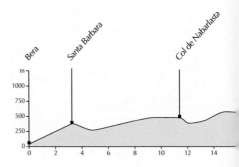

offering accommodation from 2019 (**2hr 30min**, 440m, N43°15.636 W001°37.147).

Keep straight on up the hill ahead to reach a col (**2hr 40min**, 475m). The GR11 goes right and descends unnecessarily, so you should leave it here and continue along the track. A small bothy with picnic table is above you on the right. Pass a col with borderstone 45 and a second col, Domikusantz (475m) to arrive at the **Col de Nabarlasta** (**3hr 5min**, 477m, N43°15.268 W001°36.000) with borderstone 50.

*Borderstone 50,
Col de Nabarlasta*

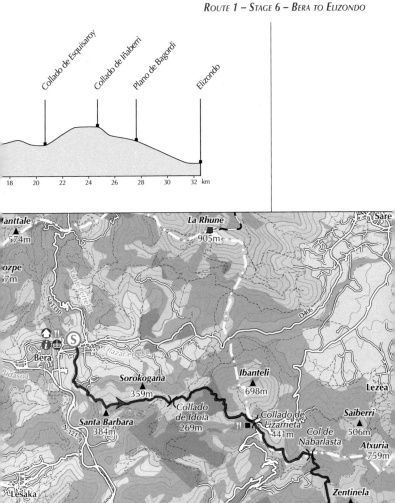

Map continues
on page 60

Turn right, signed to Elizondo, and descend, soon turning left to rejoin the GR11. Fork right, cross a stream at the bottom of the hill and turn right. Pass below a large barn then go left through the farmyard with a water point that is usually well-protected with loose dogs! Don't miss a sharp right turn 15min later and arrive at a picnic site with a water point (**3hr 35min**, 440m).

Fork left at the picnic area. The track veers right, after which you ignore right turns and continue straight to the top of the hill, then stay on the main track past a barn (**4hr**, 565m) and veer left round Zentinela (669m). Then fork left on a grassy path to rejoin the main track and immediately fork right. Pass a barn at the Collado de Irazako (530m) then reach a power-line where there is an ancient tumulus. Stay on the main track, ignoring turns, to reach a complex road junction at the **Collado de Ursumia** (**4hr 35min**, 535m, N43°14.038 W001°34.346).

Turn right (south) along a track, following the main track at a junction, then fork right at a col to start the descent. Fork left three times during the descent, then right along a path which contours through woods before joining a track just before reaching the road at **Collado de Esquisaroy** (**5hr 20min**, 506m, N43°13.010 W001°33.080). ▶

Cross the road and take the path forking right, eventually crossing the ridge and soon forking right again (**6hr**, 725m). Fork right at a junction (**5hr 35min**, 725m), then fork right and left as you continue to climb to a track joining from the left. Traverse right of Atxuela (825m) to **Collado Achuela** (**6hr 25min**, 795m) with a small

There is a sign down the road on the right to Casa Rural Landa Etxea, but at the time of writing there is no information on this possible accommodation.

Alternative accommodation for a GR11 hiker

iron cross. The track contours west of La Ronda (854m) to reach the **Collado de Iñaberri** (**6hr 35min**, 795m, 43°11.522 W001°32.141).

Turn left along the road and after about 1km fork left down a path, the first of several 'short-cuts'. Turn left on regaining the road. The next short-cut, also on the left, passes below a clay-pigeon shooting range (keep to the road if you hear shooting). Go straight across when you next meet the road, then right along the road before taking a path to the left. Cross the road when you next meet it (360m). A new well-waymarked complex descent route takes you down to a bridge under the Elizondo bypass (**8hr 10min**, 213m N43°09.012 W001°31.313). Follow the road into **Elizondo**, cross the river to reach main street and turn left to a large church on the right (**8hr 20min**, 200m). There is a water point in the churchyard.

> **Elizondo** is a small town with a seasonal tourist office and a range of accommodation. As well as smaller shops there is a large supermarket just northeast of the church.

FACILITIES FOR STAGE 6

Collado de Lizarrieta

Venta Lizaieta hopefully will offer accommodation from 2019: tel (33) 0642 52 22 80

Elizondo

Elizondo tourist office: tel (34) 948 581 517

Hotel Elizondo: tel (34) 948 580 872 https://hostalelizondo.com

Hotel Baztan: tel (34) 948 580 050

Hostal Antxitonea: tel (34) 948 581 807 www.antxitonea.com

Hostal Posada Elbete: tel (34) 948 581 519 https://posadaelbete.com

Albergue Kortarixar: tel (34) 626 532 452 www.alberguesenbaztan.com

STAGE 7
Elizondo to Aldudes

Start	Elizondo
Distance	17km
Total ascent	900m
Total descent	600m
Time	4hr 45min
High points	Col de Argibel (944m), Zarkindegi (860m)

The next accommodation along the GR11 is at least 8 hours' walking away and only open in high season, so the route leaves the GR11 at the Col de Argibel and drops down to Aldudes in France where it joins one of the more popular variations of the HRP.

In **Elizondo**, follow red/white GR11 waymarks to the right (west) of the church, veering left and right to reach a GR11 information board. Fork right up a track, soon forking right and left before rejoining the road. Follow the road for about 100 metres then turn right along a path, veering left to reach a track. Turn right and left, then right and fork left below a farmhouse. Join a track and turn right along a path as you come close to the road. Go straight across the road when you next meet it (**1hr 5min**, 440m, N43°07.343 W001°30.081). You now pass several springs; you will probably get the best water from the third, from a tiny pipe (**1hr 20min**).

Ignore a right fork as you leave the wood then turn right when you meet a good track (**1hr 35min**) and left at a second junction. You could follow the track all the way to the Collado de Urballo but the GR11 forks right (the middle path) and immediately passes 20 metres right of a good water source, **Trampako Iturria**, where camping is possible (**2hr 10min**, 704m, N43°06.096 W001°29.773). Continue up to a hunter's cabin, with

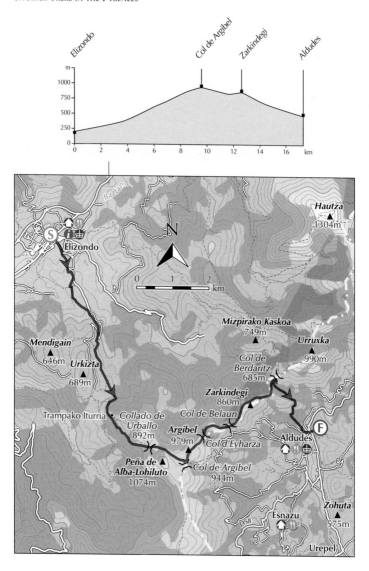

water point and picnic tables, just below the **Collado de Urballo** (**2hr 45min**, 892m, N43°05.690 W001°28.953).

Keep straight on, soon forking right for a gently rising traverse ESE on the northern slopes of Peña de Alba-Lohiluto to reach a signpost at the **Col de Argibel** (**3hr 5min**, 944m, N43°05.452 W001°28.275) at the junction between the GR11 and the GRT5.

Turn left (northeast), following the GRT5, also with red/white waymarks. Pass borderstone 126 as you skirt right of the rocky summit of **Argibel** (979m). The path veers away from the fence and descends to the **Col d'Eyharza** with borderstone 125 (**3hr 20min**, 846m). Veer slightly left, round the next top and descend to the **Col de Belaun** (**3hr 35min**, 759m, N43°06.012 W001°27.327).

The GRT5 now climbs just left of the summit of **Zarkindegi** (860m), but it's just as easy to go over the summit before dropping down to Elokadi (758m) with borderstone 119. Turn left along a good track which leads to the **Col de Berdaritz** with GRT5 information boards and borderstone 117 (**4hr 15min**, 685m, N43°06.730 W001°26.348).

Leave the GRT5 here and turn sharp right, signed to 'Aldude'. Take the descending option at every junction and the track eventually becomes a tarmac farm

Church in Aldudes

Carving on stone in Aldudes

road which takes you into the centre of **Aldudes** with bar-restaurant, chambres d'hôtes and water point (**4hr 45min**, 480m, N43°05.904 W001°25.660).

For further facilities in **Aldudes**, cross the bridge and turn right to the small store in the petrol station, Bar Alfaro and the Auberge Erreka Gorri which has recently been converted into a gîte d'étape provided by the community. Hôtel Saint Sylvestre is at Esnazu 3km to the southwest of Aldudes.

FACILITIES FOR STAGE 7

Aldudes

Gîte d'étape Auberge Erreka Gorri. Contact Bar Alfaro for details: tel (33) 0559 37 58 61 http://vallee-aldudes.com/listings/erreka-gorri

Chambres d'hôtes Mano & Michel Heguy: tel (33) 0559 37 57 68 or (33) 0676 61 37 06

Esnazu

Hôtel Saint Sylvestre: tel (33) 0559 37 58 13 www.hotel-restaurant-vallee-des-aldudes.com

See http://vallee-aldudes.com for other accommodation

STAGE 8
Aldudes to Burguete (Auritz)

Start	Aldudes
Distance	21km
Total ascent	1100m
Total descent	700m
Time	6hr 25min
High points	Otsamunho (901m), Errola (907m), Urtaray (1152m), Lindus (1220m)

This stage is a high-level traverse of a long grassy ridge following the line of the HRP. There is very little waymarking, so care will be needed with navigation.

Cross the bridge in **Aldudes** and turn right, then left up steps immediately before the petrol station. Climb steeply up a small path to reach a col, then contour right before veering left uphill and turning right along a concrete track to reach a tarmac farm road junction by a barn (**40min**, 550m, N43°05.675 W001°24.864). The route of the HRP is unclear from here but it is suggested you cross the road and follow the path going diagonally left which

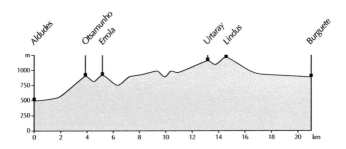

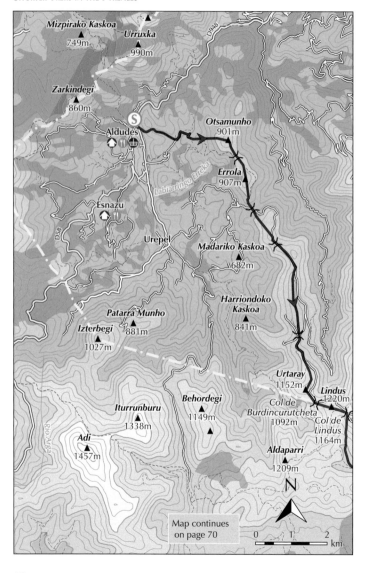

Map continues
on page 70

eventually rejoins the road by another barn (**55min**, N43°05.731 W001°24.517). Take the path straight up the hill, cross another small col and climb to reach the small summit cairn on the rocky ridge of **Otsamunho** (**1hr 40min**, 901m, N43°05.737 W001°23.718).

Descend the south-southeast ridge to reach a **col** (**1hr 50min**), then continue over **Errola** (**2hr 5min**, 907m, N43°05.129 W001°23.383) and down to a road **col** (**2hr 20min**). It is possible water will be flowing from a water-tank across the road. Continue straight up the hill on an improving track which takes you back to the road (**2hr 45min**), and follow the road up to a **col** with an excellent water point (**2hr 55min**, 925m, N43°04.064 W001°22.566). ▶

In bad weather you may prefer to follow the road all the way to the Col de Lindus.

Follow the road to the next col then fork right up the wooded ridge and continue along the ridge. Just after a grassy top (990m) pass a hunters' cabin, with picnic table, and descend to a road, also with a water point (**3hr 40min**, 957m, N43°02.828 W001°22.275).

Cross the road and continue up the north ridge of **Urtaray**, veering right to the small summit cairn (**4hr 25min**, 1152m, N43°02.018 W001°22.215). Descend southeast to the **Col de Burdincurutcheta** (1092m) with borderstone 152 and head up the ridge to **Lindus** (**5hr**,

Fortifications on Lindus

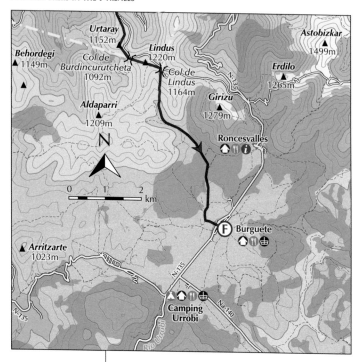

1220m, N43°01.785 W011°21.601) with a hill fort and borderstone 153.

> The **fortifications** that can be seen today date back to the wars of the invasion of Navarre by the Spanish armies of Isabel the Catholic in 1793–4 and the defence by Anglo-Spanish forces against Marshal Soult in the Napoleonic wars in 1813.

Follow the border fence ESE down to the road at the **Col de Lindus** (**5hr 10min**, 1164m, N43°01.714 W001°21.317) and borderstone 154. Leave the HRP here and head south down a path signed 'Auritz 4.9km', following yellow waymarks. (If you miss the waymarked route it should be easy enough to follow descending paths then turn left on reaching the main track at the bottom of the valley where you rejoin the GR11.) The track eventually becomes a tarmac farm road. There are picnic tables where you cross the Xubingua stream, then veer left and follow roads to the church at the centre of **Burguete** (**6hr 25min**, 894m, N42°59.362 W001°20.150). There is a water point in the churchyard.

> **Burguete** is a village with good tourist facilities to cater for Camino de Santiago walkers. Turn left up the road for Hostal Burguete and, at the top of the village, a well-stocked supermarket beside a picnic area with water and toilets. Turn right down the road for the bakery, bank, Hostal Juandeaburre and Hotel Loizu. There are also several *casas rurales* offering accommodation in the village. Camping Urrobi, which is about 2km southwest of Burguete, has a 42-bed hostel and cabins as well as camping facilities and a small shop.

FACILITIES FOR STAGE 8

Burguete

Hotel Loizu: tel (34) 948 760 008 http://loizu.com

Hostal Burguete: tel (34) 948 760 005 www.hotelburguete.com

Hostal Juandeaburre: tel (34) 948 760 078

Camping Urrobi: tel (34) 948 760 200 www.campingurrobi.com

STAGE 9
Burguete to St-Jean-Pied-de-Port

Start	Burguete
Distance	28km
Total ascent	600m
Total descent	1300m
Time	6hr 15min
High points	Col de Lepoeder (1429m)

This spectacular stage follows the Camino de Santiago along open ridges. Hundreds of 'pilgrims' will be starting from St-Jean-Pied-de-Port daily and passing through Roncesvalles and Burguete en route for Santiago. There is excellent waymarking throughout.

From the church in **Burguete**, head northeast up the main road, passing toilets with a water point and picnic area and then the supermarket. Turn left opposite the supermarket and veer right into the woods, returning to the road at **Roncesvalles** (Orreaga) (**30min**, 938m, N43°00.502 W001°19.168).

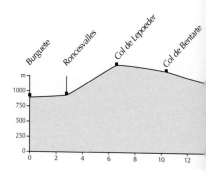

Roncesvalles has been on a transit route through the Pyrenees for thousands of years and is believed to be the route by which the Celts entered the Iberian Peninsula. Roman roads followed, and Charlemagne's army was defeated at the Battle of Roncesvalles in AD778. However, it was the 'discovery' of the tomb of St James (Sant Iago) in Galicia in 813 that soon resulted in many Christian

Sculpture commemorating the Battle of Roncesvalles

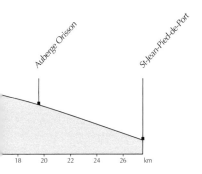

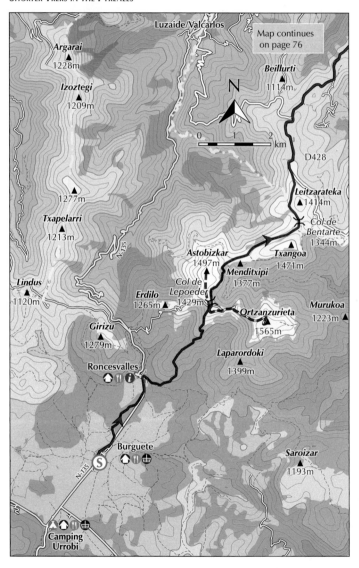

Map continues on page 76

Luzaide/Valcarlos

Argarai
▲1228m

Izoztegi
▲1209m

Beillurti
▲1114m

D428

▲1277m

Leitzarateka
▲1414m

Txapelarri
▲1213m

Col de Bentarte
1344m

N-135

Astobizkar
▲1497m

Txangoa
▲1471m

Menditxipi
▲1377m

Lindus
▲1120m

Col de Lepoeder
▲1429m

Erdilo
1265m ▲

Murukoa
1223m ▲

Ortzanzurieta
▲1565m

Girizu
▲1279m

Laparordoki
▲1399m

Roncesvalles
⌂ ⑪ ⓘ

Saroizar
▲1193m

Burguete
⌂ ⑪ ⊞

Ⓢ

N-135

⌂ ⌂ ⑪ ⊞
Camping
Urrobi

pilgrims crossing the Pyrenees en route for Santiago de Compostela. A hospital-monastery was built in the 12th century to care for pilgrims and has been enlarged on many occasions due to the increase in numbers.

The large pilgrims' hostel is reserved for those on the Camino de Santiago but there is hotel accommodation for 'tourists' as well as a tourist information office, souvenir shop, toilets, water points and guided tours.

Turn right in front of 'La Posada' and leave from the southeast corner of the main car park. Soon turn left and follow a large path climbing steeply to reach a road at the top of the woods (1405m, N43°01,538 W001°17.792). It would be possible to follow this road to the summit of Ortzanzurieta (1565m).

Cross the road and soon reach the **Col de Lepoeder** (**2hr 10min**, 1429m). ▸ The Camino de Santiago now follows a good track as it traverses the east slopes of Astobizkar, passes an emergency shelter (**2hr 30min**, N43°02.240 W001°17.314) and, after forking left at the **Col de Bentarte** (**3hr 5min**, 1344m), passes a water point, Fontaine de Roland, and continues to the D428 road (**3hr 15min**, 1230m). There will probably be a mobile snack-bar a short distance down the road.

Astobizkar, to the north (1497m), could be climbed from here.

Camping below Col de Lepoeder

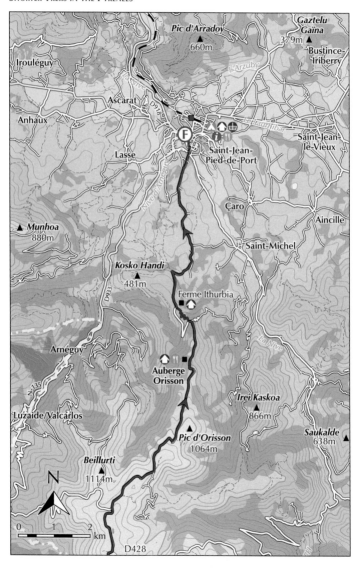

This road, with very little traffic, is followed all the way to St-Jean-Pied-de-Port. Follow the road along an open ridge and eventually pass **Auberge Orisson** with water point and gîte d'étape with hostel-style accommodation and bar-restaurant providing snacks during the day (meals for residents only in the evening) (**4hr 40min**, 810m, N43°06.527 W001°14.370).

The descent now steepens, and you turn right to shortcut a switchback. Soon after rejoining the road you pass **Ferme Ithurburia** chambres d'hôtes, with water point, which offers light refreshments.

Continue down the D428 into **St-Jean-Pied-de-Port**. Keep straight on through the gate and down a cobbled street in the old town and take the first left turn to a roundabout at the south end of town (**6hr 15min**, 227m, N43°09.791 W001°14.339) where there are toilets and a water point.

FACILITIES FOR STAGE 9

Roncesvalles

Local information: www.roncesvalles.es

Tourist office: tel (34) 948 760 301 www.turismo.navarra.es

La Posada (guest house): tel (34) 948 760 225 http://laposada.roncesvalles.es

Hotel Roncesvalles: tel (34) 948 760 105 www.hotelroncesvalles.com

Cas Sabina (guest house): tel (34) 948 760 012 http://casasabina.roncesvalles.es

Pilgrims' hostel: tel (34) 948 760 000 or (34) 948 760 029 (Note Camino de Santiago pilgrims have priority)

Descent to St-Jean-Pied-de-Port

Auberge Orisson: tel (33) 0559 49 13 03 or (33) 0681 49 79 56 http://refuge-orisson.com

Ferme Ithurburia: tel (33) 0559 37 11 17

St-Jean-Pied-de-Port

See Stage 1 for accommodation in St-Jean-Pied-de-Port

ROUTE 2

*Pic du Midi d'Ossau and the limestone peaks
of the western Pyrenees*

Start/finish	Etsaut
Distance	141km
Total ascent/descent	7900m
Time	8 stages (42hr)

The magical view of the Pic du Midi d'Ossau across Lac Gentau from the Refuge d'Ayous is the classic view of the Pyrenees, appearing on the cover of many guidebooks to the area. As far as short treks are concerned, the

Tour du Pic du Midi d'Ossau is the pick of the Pyrenean routes. Here it is combined with the most spectacular sections of the La Senda de Camille (Stages 2 to 5), through the magnificent limestone scenery on the Spanish

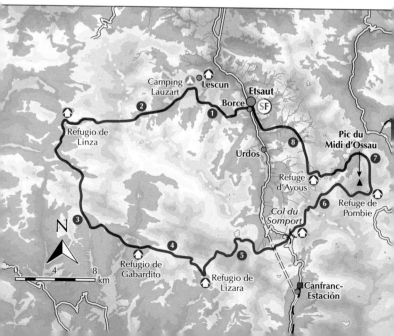

side of the border, to produce a fabulous eight-stage trek. Included is a descent of the intriguing Chemin de la Mâture, a passage hewn out of vertical limestone cliffs.

The Spanish sections of the La Senda de Camille are adequately waymarked and there is excellent waymarking on Stages 1 and 8 which follow the GR10. However, waymarking is sparse on the French section of Stage 2 and navigational skills will be required. There is little waymarking on Stages 6 and 7 but you are on well-walked paths. There is central booking for the refuges on La Senda de Camille and you can book accommodation at Lauzart, Linza, Gabardito, Lizara and Col du Somport through the website. Tel (34) 974 375 421 www.lasendade camille.com.

The French section of this route is covered by the Vallée d'Aspe tourist office in Bedous: tel (33) 05 59 34 57 57 www.tourisme-aspe.com.

Access

The obvious starting points for this route are Etsaut or the Col du Somport. There is a train service from Pau to Bedous and then a connecting bus service from Bedous to Etsaut and the Col du Somport. If approaching from Spain, take a train to Canfranc-Estación and a bus on to Col du Somport.

Shorter variations

You could split this trek by using the bus service from Etsaut to Col du Somport (Stage 6), giving a five-stage route from Etsaut to Col du Somport and a three-stage route from Col du Somport to Etsaut. This would be a good option for those who are camping as it would provide a solution to the resupply problem. Another possibility is to complete La Senda de Camille in six stages by following it from Col du Somport to Refuge d'Arlet and on to Camping du Lauzart (see Editorial Alpina map/guide to La Senda de Camille).

Maps

- *La Senda de Camille* published by Editorial Alpina at 1:25,000 covers Stages 1–5 and also gives details of the refuge on La Senda de Camille
- IGN Pyrénées Carte no 3, *Béarn* at 1:50,000 covers Stages 1–3 and 6–8

STAGE 1

Etsaut to Camping du Lauzart (Lescun)

Start	Etsaut
Distance	17km
Total ascent	1100m
Total descent	900m
Time	4hr 50min
High points	Col de Barrancq (1601m)

This stage follows the GR10 from Etsaut to Lescun with excellent red/white waymarking. For those with excess energy or time, it is worth climbing Pic de Labigouer (2175m), a wonderful viewpoint, from the Col de Barrancq.

Etsaut has the Gîte d'étape La Garbure and a bar-restaurant, Le Randonneur.

Cross the bridge at the south end of **Etsaut** (600m, N42°54.636 W000°34.257) and turn right, then left over the footbridge and climb to **Borce**. Turn left, passing several water points and toilets. Turn right past the church (keep straight on for the gîte d'étape, épicerie and bar-restaurant) and follow the clear signs and waymarks as

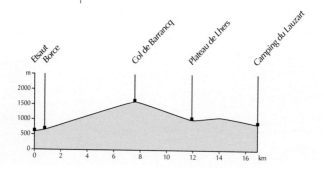

Le Randonneur, Etsaut

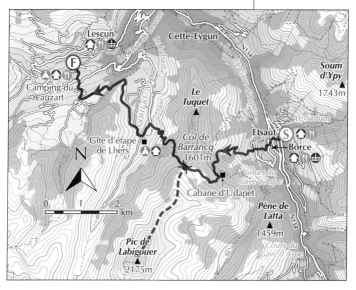

you climb steeply. Pass right of the boundary fence of the Parc d'Ours (www.parc-ours.fr), a wildlife park.

When you reach a road turn sharp right, then sharp left before resuming the steep ascent. Pass a path to Chambres d'hôtes l'Espiatet (**45min**, 860m). Cross a couple of reliable streams (1000m and 1260m) before arriving at the **Cabane d'Udapet**, a shepherds' hut with water point (**2hr 15min**, 1400m). Veer right; the path and waymarking is a little vague but you should easily reach the wooded **Col de Barrancq** (**2hr 50min**, 1601m).

> It is well worth climbing **Pic de Labigouer** (2175m), to the south-southwest (100min up, 75min down). A good second-best would be the first summit on the ridge (1913m) (up and down in 1hr).

There are plenty of camping opportunities on the descent, despite the steep gradient. Follow a well-way-marked combination of paths and tracks. Pass a spring with piped water (**3hr 20min**, 1290m), reach a road in the **Plateau de Lhers** and turn left to a road junction. The Gîte d'étape de Lhers is about 100 metres ahead, but our route goes right across the bridge (**3hr 40min**, 1000m, N42°54.710 W000°37.194).

Follow the road as it veers right then turn left up a track. At the end of the track go through a gate into the wood, contour and then veer right across a stream and between houses with a water point. Now follow a complex but well-waymarked route along paths, roads and tracks to a major road junction. ◀ Keep straight on for **Camping du Lauzart** (**4hr 50min**, 850m, N42°55.683 W000°38.498).

If you don't need the gîte d'étape or Lescun you could turn left here and start Stage 2.

> **Camping du Lauzart**, with gîte d'étape, was closed for renovation in 2018 but is expected to reopen in 2019 under new management. If it isn't open you will have to stay at Gîte d'étape de Lhers or at Lescun, which is a further 20min along the GR10. Lescun has a small shop, a range of accommodation and several bar-restaurants.

FACILITIES FOR STAGE 1

Etsaut

Gîte d'étape la Garbure: tel (33) 0559 34 88 98 www.garbure.net

Borce

Gîte le Communal: tel (33) 0559 34 86 40 www.lecommunal.fr

Chambre d'hôtes l'Espiatet: tel (33) 0750 35 89 13 www.lespiatet.com

Chambre d'hôtes Maison Bergoun: tel (33) 0642 69 47 45 www.bergoun.com

Plateau de Lhers

Gîte d'étape de Lhers: tel (33) 0559 34 75 39 or (33) 0670 20 45 86 www.gite-camping-lhers.com

End of stage

Camping du Lauzart and gîte d'étape: tel (33) 0559 34 78 80 www.camping-gite-lescun-pyrenees.com

Lescun

Gîte d'étape Maison de la Montagne offers a full meals service: tel (33) 0559 34 79 14 or (33) 0687 19 81 94

Hôtel du Pic d'Anie, chambres d'hôtes and gîte d'étape accommodation + breakfast and evening meals: tel (33) 0559 34 71 54 https://hebergement-picdanie.fr

Puerto d'Acherito

STAGE 2
Camping du Lauzart (Lescun) to Refugio de Linza

Start	Camping du Lauzart (Lescun)
Distance	20km
Total ascent	1300m
Total descent	800m
Time	6hr 5min
High points	Colláu de Petrachema (2082m)

La Senda de Camille is followed through limestone karst terrain over the Colláu de Petrachema (Puerto de Anso) with spectacular views of the Aiguille d'Ansabère. It would be easy to climb Petrachema (Pic d'Ansabère) (2371m). There is no waymarking except for occasional cairns and even rarer HRP yellow waymarks until you reach the col. It would be possible to continue down the road to Zuriza to shorten the long third stage.

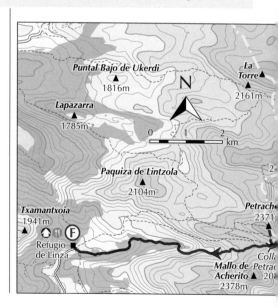

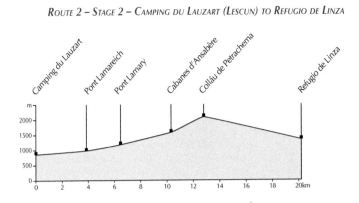

From **Camping du Lauzart** return south to the road junction and turn right following signs to Masousa-Ansabère. Stay on the 'main' road at several junctions as you gradually climb, staying left of the stream. Cross **Pont Lamareich** (**50min**, 970m, N42°54.717 W000°40.287) and follow a

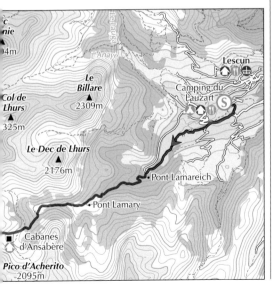

85

good track left, signed to Cabanes d'Ansabère, still along the left-hand side of the stream, to arrive at a small car park at **Pont Lamary** (**1hr 35min**, 1170m, N42°54.337 W000°41.460).

Cross the bridge and follow a smaller track through pasture and woodland up the right-hand side of the stream to the Plateau d'Ansabère, a grassy area with good camping (**2hr 20min**, 1365m, N42°54.196 W000°42.530). The track continues from the left-hand side of the grassy bowl and leads through woods to the **Cabanes d'Ansabère** (**2hr 55min**, 1570m, N42°53.888 W000°42.983) with a shepherd's private cabin and a smaller bothy. The water point will probably provide your last water until you are approaching the Refugio de Linza.

Follow the faint path to the right of the cabins and on to a (missable) fork marked by a small cairn (**3hr 20min**, 1650m, N42°53.884, W000°43.324). Fork right and initially head directly for the towering Aiguille S d'Ansabère, which is the SW top of Petrachema (Pic d'Ansabère), then veer right before swinging back left across scree and boulderfield to the **Colláu de Petrachema** (**4hr 20min**, 2082m, N42°53.885 W43.984). In early season there will be snowfields on the approach to the col. ◀

The ascent of Petrachema (2371m) to the right is straightforward.

You now start picking up the green/yellow waymarks of La Senda de Camille, supplemented by cairns. There are two cairned paths going roughly west from the col; the right-hand is the Camino de Francia Petrachema which takes a higher route and the left is the route of La Senda de Camille which goes down the valley. Take the left path and descend through limestone karst and eventually drop into a grassy sinkhole (**5hr 15min**, 1630m) with the first obvious campsite since the Cabanes d'Ansabère, but still no water. If you want to camp, it is better to continue 20min through the wood to where a stream emerges (only trickling in August 2017). Ten minutes after this, by which time the path has become a track, fork right down a path (**5hr 50min**, 1419m, N42°53.808 W000°47.279) which stays close to the stream. Cross the stream at a picnic site with an open shelter, and soon arrive at the **Refugio de Linza**, at the roadhead (**6hr 5min**, 1340m, N42°53.888 W000°47.986).

FACILITIES FOR STAGE 2
Refugio de Linza: tel (34) 974 348 289 www.refugiodelinza.com

STAGE 3
*Refugio de Linza to
Refugio de Gabardito*

Start	Refugio de Linza
Distance	26km
Total ascent	1600m
Total descent	1600m
Time	8hr 20min
High points	Above Achar d'Alano (1920m), Colláu de Lenito Baxo (1714m), Refugio de Gabardito (1380m)

The trek continues to follow La Senda de Camille through magnificent limestone scenery. This long stage could be shortened by staying at the facilities at Zuriza or Puen de Santana. Some of the waymarking is sparse and care will be needed with navigation in poor weather.

From **Refugio de Linza**, descend the road, passing a water point (15min), and arrive at **Camping Zuriza** (**55min**, 1225m, N42°51.940 W000°48.683). ▸ Turn left along the GR11, up the main track along the north side of the Barranco Petraficha. Pass Fuente Fría, a spring emerging from beneath a boulder, and several small streams to reach a car park (**1hr 30min**, 1270m, N42°51.275 W000°47.314).

The GR11 forks left, but instead cross the bridge and follow the GR11-1, with red/white waymarks, and take the path left, signed 'Achar de Alano'. There is a

There is small swimming hole under the bridge about 300 metres west along the road.

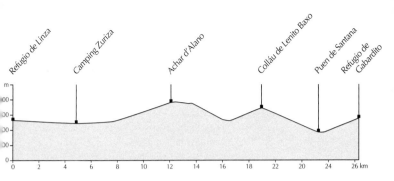

Refugio de Linza — Camping Zuriza — Achar d'Alano — Colláu de Lenito Baxo — Puen de Santana — Refugio de Gabardito

spring-fed water pipe at the start of the ascent. The path crosses the track several times before arriving to the right of a large barn. Continue climbing, or follow the track right, to arrive right of a second barn. Follow the track to a signpost at a sharp bend (**2hr 20min**, 1510m, N42°50.809, W000°46.947), just beyond the barn.

Leave the GR11-1 here and keep straight on up the hill aiming for the left-hand notch in the skyline. There

Camping below Sierra d'Alano

are good campsites just above the track and the stream to the east may be running. The nebulous path improves to a cairned mountain path which leads easily to a very easy scramble up rocks just left of the gully to arrive at a false col, **Achar d'Alano** (**3hr 30min**, 1900m, N42°50.319 W000°47.086), where a stream should be running until the end of snowmelt. ◄

Look out for chamois and marmots.

Climb a little further across a grassy plateau, ignoring a path to the left. The path is faint, but there are occasional green/yellow waymarks. The path veers left and descends gently to a small shepherds' hut, which may be available as a bothy (1870m, N42°49.977 W000°46.992). Head south across karst terrain and start the descent (N42°49.765 W000°47.000) down a dry valley on a faint rough path, marked by cairns. Eventually reach a basic bothy, with trickling streams and camping (**4hr 35min**, 1365m, N42°48.914 W000°48.738).

Keep descending and soon reach a good track. Turn left and, after about 400 metres, turn left again up a faint path, signed to 'Colláu de Lenito Baxo' (**4hr 45min**, 1295m). Waymarking improves and the path becomes clearer as it enters the wood and climbs, passing a possibly dry stream, with campsites, in a grassy bowl a little higher. The path enters the woods on the right and climbs to the grassy **Colláu de Lenito Baxo** with exposed campsites (**5hr 50min**, 1714m, N42°48.617 W000°45.590).

Descend directly down the dry valley, initially marked by two posts; a path is developing now and the descent is better waymarked, leading to another bothy (**6hr 10min**, 1470m, N42°48.333 W000°45.024). Camping is possible but there are only dubious-quality springs nearby.

Keep descending to reach a steep rough track (the good waymarking ends and you should ignore yellow/white waymarks), which you follow all the way down to the road (**7hr**, 960m, N42°47.839 W000°43.949). Turn right to a junction. Hotel Usón is about 500 metres further down the road. Turn left and cross the **Puen de Santana**, the bridge high above the Rio Aragon Subordán. You are now back on the GR11-1 with red/white waymarking.

Follow the road right for about 400 metres then turn left up a path into the woods, signed to 'Gabardito'. If you want Albergue Borda Bisaltico, which has a hostel, campground and bar-restaurant, you should continue along the road. The path shortcuts the switchbacks in the road. There is a good water point, Fuente de Balandin, at the first road crossing (**7hr 30min**). The path crosses the road five more times before arriving at the **Refugio de Gabardito** (**8hr 20min**, 1380m, N42°47.241 W000°42.692) in meadows.

Refugio de Gabardito is a modern refuge, open June to September.

FACILITIES FOR STAGE 3

Zuriza

Camping de Zuriza: tel (34) 974 370 196 www.campingzuriza.es

End of stage

Hotel Usón: tel (34) 974 375 358 www.hoteluson.com

Albergue Borda Bisaltico: tel (34) 974 348 940 www.bordabisaltico.com

Refugio de Gabardito: tel (34) 974 375387 www.alberguesyrefugiosdearagon.com

STAGE 4
Refugio de Gabardito to Refugio de Lizara

Start	Refugio de Gabardito
Distance	11km
Total ascent	700m
Total descent	500m
Time	3hr 5min
High points	Colláu de la Foratón (2014m)

This stage follows the GR11-1, which coincides with La Senda de Camille, and has good red/white waymarking. It is a short easy stage and you would have time to climb Bisaurin (2670m) or Puntal Alto del Foratón (2154m) from the Collàu de la Foratón.

The streams on the plateau may dry up in a hot summer and in this cow country any water will need treating.

From **Refugio de Gabardito** take the track ESE, signed 'Bisaurin' and follow it, ignoring numerous side-turns. The track has become a path by the time it follows a ledge cut into the near-vertical limestone cliffs, after which a signed junction is reached (**35min**, 1530m). Fork right, signed Foratón and GR11-1, and climb above the cliffs to reach a grassy plateau, Plan de Dios Te Salve (1610m). ◀

Cross a small stream and continue first past a small bothy, Refugio de Dios Te Salve (**1hr 5min**, 1650m, N42°47.050 W000°41.122) with stream and then a shepherds' hut, above the path. The ascent steepens to reach a broad col on the north ridge of Peak 2134 in the Sierra de Gabas. Now a rising traverse takes you to the **Collàu de la Foratón (2hr 25min**, 2014m, N42°46.618 W000°38.995).

Sheep being driven towards Refugio de Gabardito

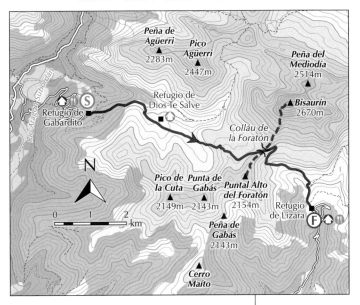

Bisaurin (2670m), the dominating peak to the NNE, is a popular climb; relatively easy but with a steep section near the top. **Puntal Alto del Foratón** (2154m) to the southwest is easy (up and down in 40min).

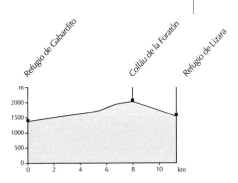

Puntal Alto del Foratón

To continue on the main route, descend left on a multi-stranded path which switchbacks down the slope, passing a possible spring and reaching a track end (1700m, N42°46.335 W000°38.310). Pass the excellent water point, Fuente de Fuenfría, and reach a junction (**3hr 5min**), signed to Ibón de Estanés. If you don't need the refuge, turn left and start Stage 5, otherwise continue down the track to the **Refugio de Lizara** (**3hr 15min**, 1540m, N42°45.832 W000°38.036) which is a modern refuge.

FACILITIES FOR STAGE 4

Refugio de Lizara: tel (34) 974 348 433 www.refugiodelizara.com

STAGE 5
Refugio de Lizara to Col du Somport

Start	Refugio de Lizara
Distance	20km
Total ascent	900m
Total descent	800m
Time	6hr 10min
High points	Puerto de Vernera (2115m), Puerto de Estanés (1792m), Col de Bessata (1683m)

The trek continues along La Senda de Camille through a terrain with towering limestone cliffs. After crossing the Puerto de Vernera you descend a north-facing slope where snow can linger well into summer and the route crosses the Gave d'Aspe which can be impossible during snowmelt (an alternative route is described).

Initially you are following the new route of the GR11 north over the Puerto de Vernera with good red/white waymarking, but green/yellow waymarking is sparse on the second half of the stage as you follow La Senda de Camille along the old route of the GR11 to Candanchú. Camping opportunities and water are frequent, but you are in cow country so the water may need treating. Instead of following La Senda de Camille, it may be possible to follow the new high-level route of the GR11 east from Lizara to Candanchú. This route had only just been waymarked in 2018 and paths were only starting to be developed.

Return to the junction above **Refugio de Lizara** and turn right, signed for Ibón de Estanés. Pass the **Refugio de Ordelca** (**30min**, 1700m, N42°46.262 W000°37.749), a small bothy, and gradually veer left into the Ordelca valley. Often high above the stream, keep climbing to reach another small bothy (**1hr 35min**, 1960m, N42°47.007 W000°37.008) and soon arrive at a magnificent 'hidden valley' named after Paúl de Vernera. Cross the stream and climb the right-hand side of the valley to your right (chamoix are often seen here) to arrive at the ill-defined

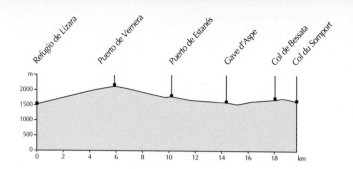

Puerto de Vernera (**2hr 10min**, 2115m, N42°46.951 W000°36.065).

Descend, gradually veering left, into Valle de los Sarrios, another 'hidden valley', and exit at the far end of the grassy area (**2hr 30min**, 2000m, N42°47.376 W000°35.336). The descent is well to the right of the stream, which falls over waterfalls, and takes you into a smaller 'hidden valley' (1920m). Turn left and descend beside the stream to reach an unsigned path junction (**2hr 50min**, 1850m, N42°47.602 W000°35.581). ◄

This junction can be buried under a snow bridge well into summer.

Ibón de Estanés

Turn right, leaving the GR11, and follow green/yellow waymarks down a complex route to the southeast tip of **Ibón de Estanés** (**3hr 15min**, 1760m). (The best campsites and swimming spots are from the rocky area on the east shore of the lake.) From the lake, head east to the **Puerto de Estanés** (**3hr 20min**, 1792m, N42°47.808 W000°35.007).

Keep straight on down a well-trod path before crossing a small stream. Go up a slight rise on the right and almost immediately turn right at an easily missed junction (**3hr 40min**, 1665m, N42°47.948 W000°34.107) for a traverse below the cliffs of the Cirque d'Aspe.

> During snowmelt, when the **Gave d'Aspe** may be uncrossable, you could keep straight on here, descend to Parking de Sansanet and then climb the main road and G65-3 (Camino de Santiago) to the Col du Somport.

Pass borderstone 293 on a knoll on the left, enter France and the woods, cross a steep stream and soon

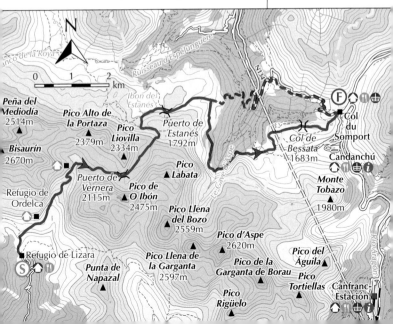

arrive at a second stream, the **Gave d'Aspe** (**4hr 25min**, 1600m). The Gave d'Aspe should be benign – even dry – in summer, but in early-season snowmelt it can be uncrossable. Cross to the lower path (the old upper path is very dangerous), leave the wood and arrive at a sign-post in meadows (**5hr 10min**). Assuming the small stream is running, it will be your last opportunity to camp beside water before the Col du Somport.

Keep straight on towards Candanchú. About 7min later, fork left at a vague unsigned junction (N42°47.199 W000°33.093) and follow yellow/green waymarks on a nebulous path which twists and turns. ◄ In mist, you will be doing very well if you can keep to the path as you climb to the right of small peaks to arrive at the **Col de Bessata** (**5hr 45min**, 1683m, N42°47.573 W000°32.308) with borderstone 300. Turn right over Peak 1726 to borderstone 303 where you turn left for the **Col du Somport** and Albergue Aysa (**6hr 10min**, 1631m, N42°47.735 W000°31.499).

In bad weather you may prefer to fork right to Candanchú and then climb the road to the Col du Somport.

Albergue Aysa has accommodation, bar-restaurant and a small shop with limited food supplies.

FACILITIES FOR STAGE 5

Albergue Aysa: tel (34) 974 373 023 www.albergueaysa.com

STAGE 6
Col du Somport to Refuge de Pombie

Start	Col du Somport
Distance	16km
Total ascent	1300m
Total descent	900m
Time	5hr 40min
High points	Col des Moines (2168m), Col de Peyreget (2315m)

Stages 6 and 7 almost circumnavigate the Pic du Midi d'Ossau and provide fantastic views of this iconic peak which dominates the area. Care is needed with navigation as there is little waymarking and a plethora of paths made by the many hikers who are attracted to the area.

From the **Col du Somport** take the road to Astún, forking left to reach the far end of the ski resort. There is no accommodation in summer, but a bar-restaurant is likely to be open in July and August.

Cross the stream and follow a clear path north up the right-hand bank to reach the shallow **Ibón del Escalar** (**1hr 30min**, 2078m). Head round the right-hand shore and climb roughly northeast to the **Col des Moines** (**1hr 50min**, 2168m, N42°49.467 W000°29.947) and enter France to be greeted with a fantastic view of the Pic du Midi d'Ossau. ▶

You now join the Chemin d'Ossau, the GR108, with occasional red/white waymarks. Veer left and soon fork right at a small knoll and descend gently. Fork right after crossing a stream (**2hr 10min**, 2000m, N42°50.017 W000°29.514), then pass a sinkhole and **Lac Castrau** and continue the descent to a track by the **Cabanes de la Hosse**.

There is a good path up Pic des Moines (2349m) to the north.

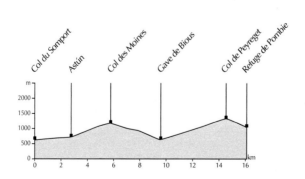

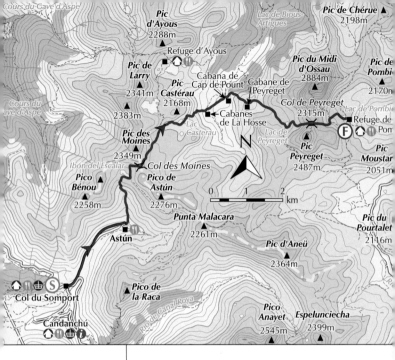

Go straight across to a bridge over the Gave de Bious (**2hr 45min**, 1644m, N42°50.354 W000°28.386), cross the bridge and follow the stream downstream. Pass left of **Cabana de Cap de Pount**, cross a small stream and immediately fork right off the path and climb towards the obvious gap in the cliffs. You soon pick up a clear path which you follow up the ridge. Pass the **Cabane de Peyreget** (N42°50.339 W000°27.671), which has a water point (only just running in August 2017) and a small room available to hikers.

Peyreget (2487m) to the right is an easy peak and a fine viewpoint.

Veer left to reach a bigger path (**3hr 45min**, 1910m), turn right and follow the path to the shallow **Lac de Peyreget** (**4hr 15min**, 2074m, N42°50.066 W000°26.933). Head round the right-hand side of the tarn and follow the cairned route east up a path and boulderfield to reach the **Col de Peyreget** (**5hr 10min**, 2315m, N42°50.054 W000°50.054). ◀

Refuge de Pombie

Descend east from the col. In late summer, the first small lake (2215m), a little right of the main path, is one of the best swimming lakes in the Pyrenees. Continue down past a second small lake and down to the Lac de Pombie with the **Refuge de Pombie** (**5hr 40min**, 2031m, N42°50.135, W000°25.623) on the east shore. There is an aire de bivouac, and swimming is possible in the lake.

FACILITIES FOR STAGE 6

Refuge de Pombie: tel (33) 0559 05 31 78 https://refugedepombie.ffcam.fr

STAGE 7
Refuge de Pombie to Refuge d'Ayous

Start	Refuge de Pombie
Distance	14km
Total ascent	700m
Total descent	800m
Time	3hr 35min
High points	Col de Suzon (2127m), Refuge d'Ayous (1965m)

This is a short easy stage but it provides the best views in the Pyrenees, and an overnight stay at Refuge d'Ayous (book ahead), or its aire de bivouac, will be an unforgettable experience.

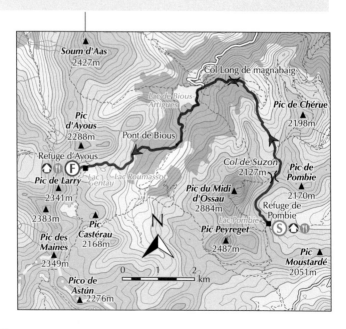

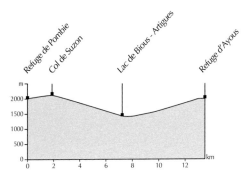

From **Refuge de Pombie** follow the path northwest, initially over a boulderfield, then veer right to climb to the **Col de Suzon** (**40min**, 2127m, N42°50.829 W000°25.404).

> The **'easy' route up Pic du Midi d'Ossau** is graded F+ and heads up the ridge to the left. It is described in Kev Reynolds' Cicerone guide *Walks and Climbs in the Pyrenees*: '…a varied ascent that involves moderate scrambling. Helmets are recommended on account of the very loose rock encountered and the fact that the way leads through gullies where stones could be dislodged by parties above.'

Descend right, eventually crossing the main stream and veering left into the woods to contour to the **Col Long de Magnabaig** (1665m). From here the path switchbacks down the steep slopes to the large car park at the east tip of **Lac de Bious-Artigues** (**1hr 50min**, 1422m, N42°52.114 W000°26.895) with toilets, cafés, canoe hire, pony trekking and a high-season bus service.

The GR10 is now followed all the way to Etsaut with excellent red/white waymarking. Follow the track along the south shore of the lake then fork left (the right fork leads to the aire de bivouac and swimming on the west shore of the lake). Follow the track as it climbs to **Pont de Bious** (**2hr 20min**, 1550m) where the northeast tip

Pic du Midi d'Ossau over Lac Gentau from Refuge d'Ayous

of a flat valley is reached. Fork right, signed for Refuge d'Ayous, and climb through woods and then hill pasture to **Lac Roumassot** (1845m) where swimming is possible. Continue well right of Lac de Miey and reach a junction overlooking **Lac Gentau** (**3hr 30min**, 1965m, N42°51.00 W000°29.240). The right fork is the route for Stage 7, but fork left and soon reach the **Refuge d'Ayous** (**3hr 35min**).

> **Refuge d'Ayous** is one of the busiest refuges in the Pyrenees and booking is essential. The view of Pic du Midi d'Ossau across Lac Gentau is a classic. It is also possible to enjoy that view from the grassy flats on the northwest shore of the lake where bivouacking is allowed, and swimming is excellent.

FACILITIES FOR STAGE 7

Refuge d'Ayous: tel (33) 0559 05 37 00 www.refuge-ayous.com

STAGE 8
Refuge d'Ayous to Etsaut

Start	Refuge d'Ayous
Distance	17km
Total ascent	300m
Total descent	1600m
Time	3hr 55min
High points	Col d'Ayous (2185m)

The final stage of this trek follows the GR10 on a long descent from the Col d'Ayous to Etsaut, including the spectacular Chemin de la Mâture – a path that was cut into a near-vertical rockface in the 17th century.

From **Refuge d'Ayous** return to the junction near the end of Stage 7 and turn sharp left to follow a clear path to the **Col d'Ayous** (**35min**, 2185m, N42°51.110 W000°29.829). ▶

Descend left, and then right at a small col, and eventually reach the valley floor (**1hr 5min**, 1890m). Continue down the left-hand side of the valley, crossing

Pic d'Ayous (2288m), to the right, is an easy peak (up and down in 25min).

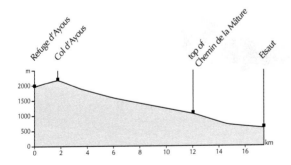

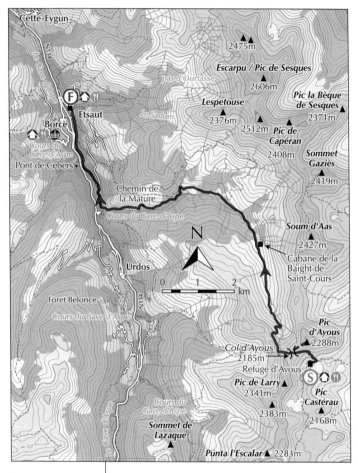

to the right before reaching **Cabane de la Baight de Saint-Cours** (1560m), a herdsman's cabin. Cross a sidestream (1490m) and a bridge over a major stream (1250m). Fork left at a sign and right at the next junction to reach the top of the **Chemin de la Mâture** (**2hr 55min**, 1065m).

Chemin de la Mâture

The **Chemin de la Mâture** was hewn out of the limestone cliffs in the 17th century to transport timber, required for the French Navy, through the Sescoué ravine.

The ledges were designed for ox-carts carrying timber so, although exposed, shouldn't present any difficulty for the walker. Descend easily to the road (**3hr 30min** 715m) and fork left along the road, staying right of the river at **Pont de Cebers** (640m) to reach the top of **Etsaut**. Keep straight on to the centre of the village (**3hr 55min**, 600m).

FACILITIES ON STAGE 8

See Stage 1 for details of accommodation and facilities in Etsaut and Borce.

ROUTE 3

Tour de Vignemale and
La Alta Ruta de Los Perdidos

Start/finish	Cauterets
Distance	186km
Total ascent/descent	10,600m
Time	11 stages (64hr)

This is a magnificent high-level trek around Vignemale and Monte Perdido, combining sections of the GR10, GR11 and HRP and featuring six of the 'honeypots' of the Pyrenees; Cauterets, Vignemale, Gavarnie, Pineta, Ordesa and the Picos del Infierno.

Deep alpine valleys and canyons, high snow-covered passes, steep cliffs, mountains with the biggest glaciers in the Pyrenees, waterfalls, cascading streams and mountain tarns make this the most spectacular but also the most demanding walk in this guide. There is 'easy' scrambling at the maximum difficulty most walkers would contemplate with a heavy pack. Some of the passes, which can hold snow well into summer, are serious undertakings until the snow has melted. In particular the Brèche de Tuquerouye (Stage 4) would present a serious risk before snowmelt. Unless you are experienced and suitably equipped for snow and ice conditions you would be advised not to attempt the route before July in a low snow year or August in a high snow year. It

is strongly advised to do the walk in a clockwise direction, as described in this guide, as the descents from Collado de Añisclo and Brèche de Tuquerouye would be very difficult when heavily laden.

On several stages you will pass refuges during the day, allowing the stages to be split into two and giving time to explore the surrounding mountains or climb some of the easier peaks. This area is extremely busy during July and August and you should book accommodation as far in advance as possible. There are plenty of opportunities for spectacular wild campsites throughout the trek.

Access

If you are approaching from France, the obvious starting points for the walk are Cauterets or Gavarnie (Stage 3) with good bus services connecting with the French rail network. From Lourdes there are buses to Argelès-Gazost with connections to Cauterets, Barèges and Gavarnie. Access is slightly more difficult on the Spanish

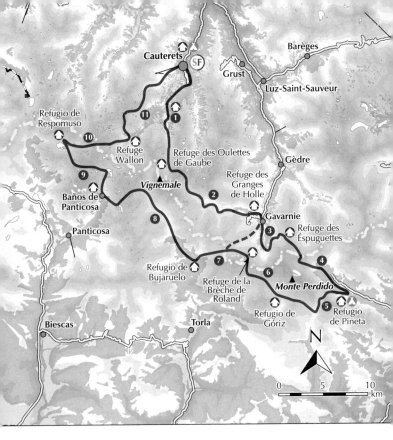

side, but you could start in Ordesa (Torla), Baños de Panticosa (Stage 9) or Pineta (Stage 5). Ordesa is a tourist hotspot and can be accessed by bus from major cities in Catalonia.

Shorter alternatives

This route is designed so it is easy to split into two separate walks – the Tour of Vignemale (7 stages) and Tour de Monte Perdido (5 stages) – using the Port de Boucharo between Gavarnie and the Refugio de Bujaruelo. This may be convenient for those who are wild-camping as it could ease resupply. There are many other possible variations.

Maps

- IGN Pyrénées Carte no 4, *Bigorre* at 1:50,000 covers Stages 1–4 and 6–11

* *La Alta Ruta de Los Perdidos*
  published by Editorial Alpina at   1:30,000 covers Stages 2–7

ALTERNATIVE ROUTES

Tour of Vignemale (7 stages)

Follow Stages 1, 2 and the early part of 3 from Cauterets to Gavarnie then follow the linking stage from Gavarnie to Refugio de Bujaruelo:

From the Vival supermarket in the middle of **Gavarnie** head up the Chemin d'Espagne and immediately right up a cobbled road. This soon becomes a path; follow signs to Port de Bouchara at several junctions and climb to reach the Plateau de Bellevue. There is a bothy above the path (N42°43.200 W000°01.036). Fork right at a signpost (**1hr 5min**, 1661m, N42°43.107 W000°01.057) and climb gently to enter the Vallée de Pouey-Aspé. Cross a small stream with good camping (**1hr 50min**, 1860m). Pass the Cabane des Soldats, a bothy (**2hr 15min**, 1950m, N42°42.631 W000°02.697). Before you reach a large fallen block, a faint path switchbacks right (**2hr 35min**) to climb to the path along the side of the valley to reach the **Port de Boucharo** (**3hr 20min**, 2270m, N42°42.236 W000°03.857) where you join Stage 7 for the descent to the **Refugio de Bujaruelo** (**5hr**).

Now follow Stages 8–11 to return to **Cauterets**.

Tour of Monte Perdido (5 stages)

This tour follows Stages 3–6 of Route 3 with a connection between Refuge de la Brèche de Roland and Gavarnie. If you are approaching from France, Gavarnie would be the most convenient starting point for this trek.

Starting from **Gavarnie**, walk Stages 3–6 of the main trek, then follow Stage 7 from **Refuge de la Brèche de Roland** to **Port de Bouchara** (**1hr**). Head about 50 metres down the main track then turn right down a small signed path which switchbacks down to the valley floor. Follow the path along the left-hand side of the valley, past the Cabane des Soldats (**1hr 35min**), a small bothy. The path eventually rises high above the stream and veers left into the Plateau de Bellevue, with a bothy (N42°43.200 W000°01.036). Turn left at a signpost (**2hr 10min**) and continue down to the path to the centre of **Gavarnie** (**2hr 45min**).

STAGE 1
Cauterets to Refuge des Oulettes de Gaube

Start	Cauterets
Distance	21km
Total ascent	1400m
Total descent	200m
Time	6hr 35min
High points	Refuge des Oulettes de Gaube (2151m)

This stage follows the GR10, with good red/white waymarking, along paths which are understandably very popular with tourists. Dramatic cataracts and waterfalls in the Val de Jéret are followed by the approach up the Vallée de Gaube to the spectacular north face of Vignemale. The stage could be split by staying at the Refuge du Clot from where it would be easy to continue on to Refuge Baysselance in Stage 2.

> **Cauterets** has all the facilities you would expect of a major tourist resort with a good range of accommodation, of which only a small selection is given in the facilities section. Catena ironmongers stocks all types of camping gas. Gîte d'étape le Cluquet provides the most basic and cheapest accommodation and also accepts small tents. There are seven campgrounds to the north of town. There are bus connections to Lourdes, Luz-Saint-Sauveur and Gavarnie and a shuttle bus service to Pont d'Espagne.

Head east from the tourist office in the centre of **Cauterets** (930m, N42°53.323 W000°06.869) and go diagonally left up the Allée du Parc to reach les Bains du Rocher and Thermes de César. Go between these two spa resorts and follow a path behind the Thermes de César. Continue on the excellent path which switchbacks up the hill before going straight across a road. Veer right past a water

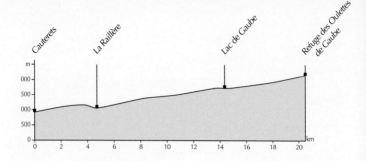

point and climb gently, high above the river, until you reach a path junction (1150m). Fork right and descend to the bridge across the Cascade du Lutour. Cross and fork right to **La Raillère** (**1hr 10min**, 1050m, N42°52.338 W000°06.569) with a number of bar-restaurants and souvenir shops.

> As you approach La Raillère you will notice a strong sulphurous odour from the **natural hot springs** which are exploited by the Thermes de Griffons (https://thermesdecauterets.com).

Cross the bridge over the river and follow the well-trod path up the right-hand side of the **Val de Jéret**. Pass two bridges and some magnificent waterfalls before turning right up a paved path to reach the **Hôtellerie du Pont d'Espagne** with hotel accommodation and bar-restaurant (**3hr 10min**, 1500m, N42°51,060 W000°08.396).

> The **Refuge du Clot** (N42°51.103 W000°08.820) and an aire de bivouac are set in lovely meadows about 10min up the road to the right of the hotel. There are public toilets and an information office at the huge car park just below the Pont d'Espagne from where there is a shuttle bus service to Cauterets.

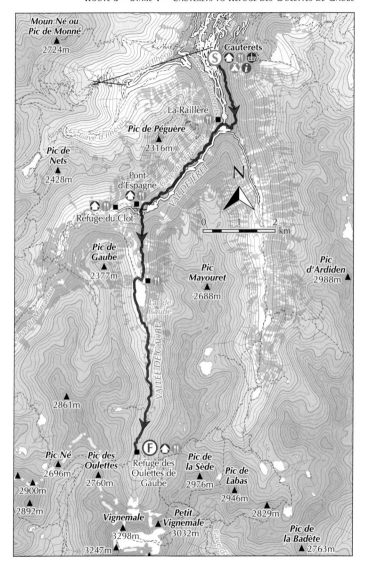

113

The north face of Vignemale from Oulettes de Gaube

FACILITIES FOR STAGE 1

Cauterets

Tourist office: tel (33) 0562 92 50 50 www.cauterets.com

Only a small selection of the accommodation in Cauterets is listed here.

Gîte d'étape Beau Soleil: tel (33) 0562 92 53 52 or (33) 0684 22 49 37

Gîte d'étape le Pas de l'Ours: tel (33) 0562 92 58 07 www.lepasdelours.com

Gîte d'étape le Cluquet: tel (33) 0674 81 66 22 http://gite-lecluquet-cauterets.com

Hôtel Christian: tel (33) 0562 92 50 04 www.hotel-christian.fr

Hôtel le Lion d'Or: tel (33) 0562 92 52 87 http://hotel-cauterets.fr/fr

Camping la Prairie: tel (33) 0562 92 07 04 http://campinglaprairie.over-blog.com

Pont d'Espagne

Hôtellerie du Pont d'Espagne: tel (33) 0562 92 54 10 www.hotel-du-pont-despagne.fr

Chalet-refuge du Clot: tel (33) 0562 92 61 27 http://www.refuge-clot.csvss.fr/fr

Oulettes de Gaube

Refuge des Oulettes de Gaube: tel (33) 0562 92 62 97 www.refugeoulettes degaube.ffcam.fr

Cross the Pont d'Espagne and take the road down the right-hand side of the gorge. After 100 metres turn right up a 'tourist path' and follow this to the **Lac de Gaube** (**4hr 20min**, 1725m). There is a bar-restaurant with public toilets and water point at the north tip of the lake. The best swimming and campsites are at the south end of the lake.

Head along the west shore of the lake and continue up the right-hand side of the valley before crossing the stream on a bridge. Recross the stream at the next bridge and stay on the right-hand side of the valley at the third bridge. Finally cross the stream to arrive at the popular **Refuge des Oulettes de Gaube** with its magnificent view of the north face of Vignemale (**6hr 35min**, 2151m, N42°47.750 W000°08.482). There is an aire de bivouac on the edge of the meadows on the right-hand side of the valley.

STAGE 2

Refuge des Oulettes de Gaube to Refuge des Granges de Holle (Gavarnie)

Start	Refuge des Oulettes de Gaube
Distance	22km
Total ascent	800m
Total descent	1400m
Time	6hr 50min
High points	Hourquette d'Ossoue (2734m)

Stage 2 follows the GR10 over the Hourquette d'Ossoue to Gavarnie. This is the highest pass on the GR10 and although there will be snowfields well into summer, it is one of the easier high passes and the well-cairned route should be easy to follow. In good weather you might like to climb Petit Vignemale, one of the easiest 3000m peaks in the Pyrenees. The stage could be split by staying at the Refuge Baysselance, the highest manned refuge in the Pyrenees.

Head east from **Refuge des Oulettes de Gaube**, forking left after 50 metres, and climb a good rocky path which switchbacks up to a junction (**1hr**). Turn right and climb

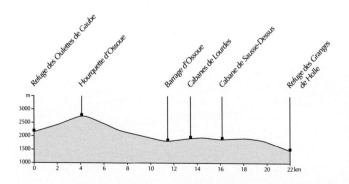

to the **Hourquette d'Ossoue** (**2hr**, 2734m, N42°46.761 W000°07.878).

> From here you can climb **Petit Vignemale** (3032m), to the right, by its northeast ridge with faint paths leading up easy rubble and rock slopes (up and down in 80min).

Contour left before switchbacking down, followed by a slight climb up a knoll to the **Refuge Baysselance** (**2hr 15min**, 2651m, N42°46.760 W000°07.450) with a rather austere aire de bivouac. ▸

The GR10 continues roughly ESE. The route is easy to follow and is surprisingly free of snow by July in an average year. Switchback down, passing the **Grottes de Bellevue** (**2hr 35min**, 2420m).

> These caves were hewn out of the rock for **Count Henry Russell**, in the 1880s, as accommodation in his exploration of Vignemale. They are still used for an uncomfortable bivouac.

The path now switchbacks steeply down, but surprisingly there are good campsites beside a stream, 10min later. Continue down the good path until you reach a boulderfield through which several meltwater streams from the Glacier d'Ossoue flow. The cairns and waymarking here can be destroyed and may be unclear in mist. You gain a little height crossing these boulderfields to pick up the path on the other side which climbs slightly as it follows a ledge cut out of the cliffs and then continues the descent. As you approach the bottom of the descent you will probably have snowfields, composed of avalanche debris, to cross well into August.

Eventually you reach a bridge across the Gave d'Ossoue at the head of the flat valley floor of the Oulettes d'Ossoue (**3hr 50min**, 1915m). Cross the bridge and follow a vague path down the left-hand side of the valley to the Barrage d'Ossoue (**4hr 5min**, 1834m,

The refuge is the base for the voie normale (Grade F) climb of Vignemale (3298m) by the Glacier d'Ossoue.

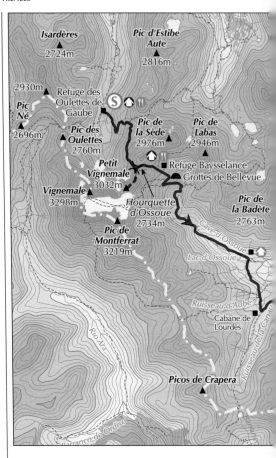

N42°45.433 W000°05.676). Swimming is possible and there is a basic bothy and aire de bivouac by the dam.

The GR10 now follows a generally rising traverse of the slopes south of the Gave d'Ossoue. There are plenty of camping opportunities and you cross a number of small streams. Start by crossing the stream on a bridge immediately below the dam and follow a path roughly

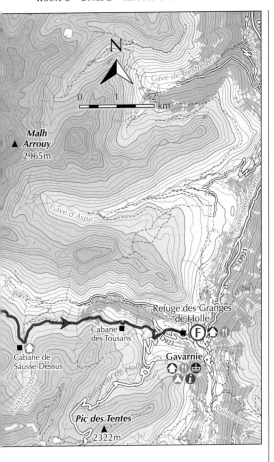

south through pasture, veering southeast then south again to pass the **Cabane de Lourdes** (**4hr 40min**, 1970m). Cross the stream flowing from the Vallée de la Canau and veer left.

Continue the traverse, passing the **Cabane de Sausse-Dessus**, a bothy in good condition in 2017 (**5hr 20min**). Cross the stream (with small rockpools) and veer left to

Barrage d'Ossoue

reach a highpoint in the traverse. There are a few ups and downs before you reach the tiny, recently restored, **Cabane des Tousaus**, which could be a useful shelter in a storm (**6hr 15min**, 1820m, N42°44.485 W000°04.268).

Veer slightly left to pick up the path, and better way-marking, and follow a little ridge before veering right and descending to the **D923** road. Go straight across, and straight across again when you the next meet the road, to arrive at the **Refuge des Granges de Holle** (**6hr 50min**, 1495m, N42°44.364 W000°01.333). Camping is possible here.

FACILITIES FOR STAGE 2

Baysselance

Refuge Baysselance: tel (33) 0974 77 66 52 or (33) 0688 29 89 60 (when refuge is closed) https://refugebayssellance.ffcam.fr

End of stage

Refuge des Grange de Holle: tel (33) 0562 92 48 77 https://chaletlagrangede-holle.ffcam.fr

Gavarnie

See Stage 3

STAGE 3

Refuge des Granges de Holle to
Refuge des Éspuguettes

Start	Refuge des Granges de Holle
Distance	10km
Total ascent	700m
Total descent	200m
Time	2hr 55min
High points	Refuge des Éspuguettes (2030m)

This short stage gives you the opportunity to enjoy the 'delights' of the tourist village of Gavarnie and explore the Cirque de Gavarnie or even climb Piméné (2801m). The recommended route via Hôtel du Cirque is far superior to the steep direct climb to the Refuge du Pailla from Gavarnie.

Follow the track down from the **Refuge des Granges de Holle**, forking left then following a path along the left-hand bank of the stream to reach a road. Turn right across the bridge then fork left down a track, then right along the

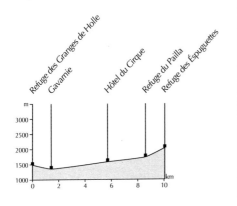

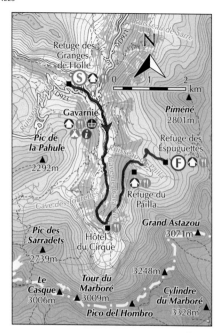

road to the tourist office at bottom of **Gavarnie**. Continue up the main street to a road junction by the Vival supermarket (**25min**, 1380m).

> **Gavarnie** is a car-free village which is one of the tourist 'honeypots' of the Pyrenees. It has all the facilities you would expect of such a place, including bar-restaurants, hotels, gîte d'étape, campsites, a small supermarket, equipment stores, tourist office, water point and toilets. There is a bus service to Luz-Saint-Sauveur and on to Lourdes and Tarbes.

From the supermarket, head up towards the Cirque de Gavarnie, crossing to the left side of the Gave de Gavarnie and following the tourist track all the way to

Hôtel du Cirque, Cirque de Gavarnie

the **Hôtel du Cirque** (**1hr 20min**, 1580m, N42°42.252 W000°00.486), now just a bar-cafeteria. ▶

Turn sharp left at the Hôtel du Cirque and follow a spectacular, but easy, path along ledges beneath often overhanging cliffs. There is a vague right fork as you come to the end of the cliffs to reach the **Refuge du Pailla** (**2hr 10min**, 1740m).

This small **refuge**, open July to September, is manned by volunteer staff who provide a full refuge service. Just beyond the refuge are excellent sheltered campsites.

Cross a (possibly dry) stream to reach a signpost (N42°43.211 E000°00.112), then follow the path uphill, fork left at a national park sign and follow the 'main' path, ignoring sheep tracks, to arrive at the **Refuge des Éspuguettes** (**2hr 55min**, 2030m, N42°43.193 E000°00.741).

It is worth walking up to the Cirque de Gavarnie and exploring this magnificent area, which claims the highest waterfall in Europe (427m).

FACILITIES FOR STAGE 3

Gavarnie

Tourist office: tel (33) 0562 92 49 10 www.valleesdegavarnie.com

A small selection of the accommodation available in Gavarnie:

Camping la Bergerie: tel (33) 0562 92 48 41 www.camping-gavarnie-labergerie.com

Gîte d'étape le Gypaète: tel (33) 0562 92 40 61 http://legypaete.pagesperso-orange.fr

Gîte d'étape Oxygène: tel 0562 92 48 23 https://gite-gavarnie.com/en

Hôtel l'Astazou: tel (33) 0562 95 12 13

Pailla

Refuge du Pailla: tel (33) 0562 51 14 50

End of stage

Refuge des Éspuguettes: (33) 0562 92 40 63

STAGE 4
*Refuge des Éspuguettes to
Refugio de Pineta*

Start	Refuge des Éspuguettes
Distance	21km
Total ascent	900m
Total descent	1700m
Time	7hr 35min
High points	Hourquette d'Alans (2430m), Brèche de Tuquerouye (2669m)
Warning	The ascent of the Brèche de Tuquerouye is steep and exposed and should not be undertaken prior to snowmelt, except by experienced climbers equipped with ice-axe and crampons.

This is a difficult stage taking you into rough terrain with spectacular views of the glaciers on the north face of Monte Perdido (3355m). The ascent of the Brèche de Tuquerouye is the most difficult in this guide and should be avoided before the end of snowmelt. Attempted before snowmelt, or during bad weather conditions, this part of the route would present a serious and potentially dangerous challenge.

Head northeast from **Refuge des Éspuguettes**, turn right at a signpost and switchback up to a junction with signpost (**40min**, 2280m, N42°43.303 E000°01.467).

From here it would be possible to keep straight on for a straightforward climb of **Piméné** (2801m), a superb viewpoint. The path skirts right of Petit Pimené and the signpost suggests a time of 1hr 30min.

The onward route switchbacks right to arrive at the **Hourquette d'Alans**, a gap in the ridge (**1hr 10min**, 2430m, N42°42.930 E000°01.689). Descend switchbacks to a junction (**1hr 15min**) and follow a smaller path gradually descending right across scree slopes. The route from the valley joins from the left (**1hr 40min**). Turn right at a path junction (**1hr 55min**, 2270m N42°42.392 02.365) where it should be possible to camp, but there is unlikely to be any water. ▶

The path left leads over the Puerto de la Lera (2466m) and then descends steeply into the Valle de Pineta.

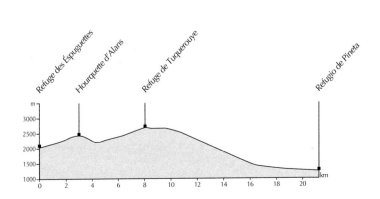

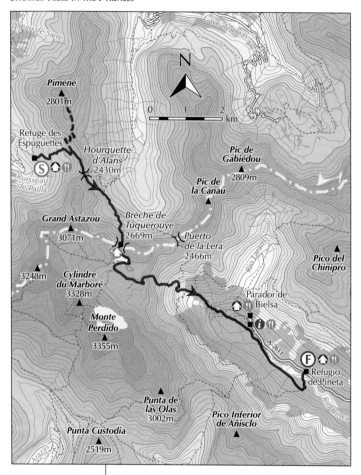

Follow the well-cairned route over bare rock and boulderfield to a small col behind a rocky peak (**2hr 40min**, 2400m) and then up a steep, awkward gully with scree and boulderfield and an exposed scramble near the top. This north-facing gully will hold snow well into summer and then the climb would only be for experienced

climbers with ice-axe and crampons. At the top of the gully you reach the **Brèche de Tuquerouye** where you'll find the Refuge de Tuquerouye, a superior bothy owned and maintained by Club Alpin Lourdes (**3hr 55min**, 2669m, N42°41.854 E000°02.404). There is a charge of €8/night (2017) for use of the bothy. There are fantastic views of the glaciers on Monte Perdido.

Glaciar de Monte Perdido

The short descent to the Lago de Marmorés is much easier, then work your way along to the left-hand end of the reservoir and back towards the dam. Here you will pick up a faint cairned path which leads into the rocky maze of the Balcón de Pineta to reach the top of the descent path (**4hr 40min**, 2550m, N42°41.342 E000°02.922). There are some spartan bivouac sites here and there is a reliable stream a few minutes down the descent path. A good mountain path switchbacks steeply down, crossing the stream three times before reaching a junction with the path descending from the Puerto de la Lera (**5hr 55min**).

Continue down to a track (**6hr 40min**). Turn right, cross a bridge over a cascading stream, pass a water point and reach the tourist office at the bottom of the descent (**7hr 5min**, 1280m, N42°40.591 E000°05.099). Here there is a water point, bar-restaurant (open in high season), large car park and toilet block. You now join the GR11 with red/white waymarking and continue through the car park and along the right-hand side of the river. Either continue to the junction with the Stage 5 ascent route or follow a signed, but not cairned, shortcut across the floodplain directly to the **Refugio de Pineta** (**7hr 35min**, 1240m, N42°39.961 E000°06.218).

Camping Pineta with cabins and a small supermarket is about 4km southeast down the road.

FACILITIES FOR STAGE 4

Refugio de Pineta: tel (34) 974 501 203 www.alberguesyrefugiosdearagon.com

Camping Pineta: tel (34) 974 501 089 www.campingpineta.com

STAGE 5
Refugio de Pineta to Refugio de Góriz

Start	Refugio de Pineta
Distance	19km
Total ascent	1900m
Total descent	1000m
Time	7hr 55min
High points	Collado de Añisclo (2453m), Collata Arrablo (2343m)

Stage 5 follows the GR11 through spectacular limestone terrain to the Refugio de Góriz at the head of the Ordesa Canyon, a World Heritage Site. There is quite a lot of easy scrambling on this stage, but the route is easier in this direction than from west to east. This is not a stage to do in bad weather and an early start is recommended to reduce the risk of being caught in afternoon thunderstorms. The Refugio de Góriz is the busiest refuge in the Spanish Pyrenees and is usually fully booked from May to October so it is essential to book as early as possible. It would be worth spending a couple of extra days at the refuge to explore the Ordesa Canyon and/or to climb Monte Perdido (3355m). National park regulations mean it is not permissible to camp between Collata Arrablo and Refugio de Góriz, but bivouac is allowed at the refuge.

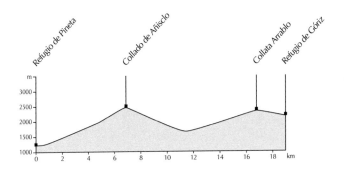

From **Refugio de Pineta** follow the cairned path, signed Añisclo, across the flood plain. Cross several strands to the river, which may be completely dry or may involve getting wet feet, to reach the junction with the GR11 at

Ascent route to Collado de Añisclo

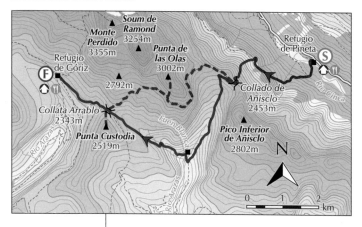

the foot of the 'wall' (N42°39.715 E000°06.162). Turn left and climb to cross a reliable stream (**50min**), then climb some easy, but exposed, rocksteps to reach a signed junction (**2hr 10min**).

Fork left to reach a small ridge at the treeline with a surprisingly reliable spring and limited camping (**2hr 20min**, 1970m, N42°39.957 E000°04.890). The climb to the ridge is well waymarked and you should take care to follow the waymarks as they find a relatively easy route up this difficult steep rocky slope. Climb to the **Collado de Añisclo** (**3hr 45min**, 2453m, N42°39.612 E000°04.579).

There are two main routes to the Refugio de Góriz from here. The high-level route, the old route of the GR11, should only be attempted by experienced mountaineers in good weather after the snow has melted. Although it is only slightly more technically difficult than the lower-level route, it is more exposed with much more potential danger. The higher route would allow an ascent of Punta de las Olas (3002m). The routes rejoin at the Collata Arrablo.

The lower-level route from Collado de Añisclo follows the new course of the GR11 and descends gently right before switchbacking down the valley, often well to the left of the Rio Bellos, to reach a bridge (**5hr 10min**, 1660m, N42°38.463 E000°03.574) with swimming holes (in September 2017 this was the last water before the end of the stage). Note Fuén Blanca emerging from the cliffs above. Turn sharp right and soon pass a small, very basic bothy.

The path heads towards **Fuén Blanca** before finding a way left through the crags. Cross the (possibly dry) stream (**5hr 55min**) and climb through a series of rocksteps well to the left of the stream to reach the **Collata Arrablo** (**7hr 20min**, 2343m, N42°39.259 E000°01.944) and follow the path roughly northwest to the **Refugio de Góriz** (**7hr 55min**, 2160m, N42°39.793 E000°00.915) and aire de bivouac.

Youth group on descent from Collata Arrablo

You can't leave a tent up during the day in the bivouac area but lockers are available in the refuge if you want to explore the **Ordesa Canyon** or climb **Monte Perdido** (3355m). Graded F, the ascent of Perdido will be relatively straightforward towards the end of summer when the snow has melted but will involve steep snow slopes earlier in the summer.

FACILITIES FOR STAGE 5

Refugio de Góriz: tel (34) 974 341 201 www.goriz.es

STAGE 6
Refugio de Góriz to
Refuge de la Brèche de Roland

Start	Refugio de Góriz
Distance	9km
Total ascent	800m
Total descent	400m
Time	3hr 30min
High points	Cuello de Millaris (2457m), Collado del Descargador (2498m), Brèche de Roland (2807m)

This is another short stage as you cross the remarkable gash of the Brèche de Roland at the western side of the Cirque de Gavarnie. It would be easy to climb Le Taillon (3144m) from here. The glacier that once used to exist between the Brèche de Roland and the Refuge de la Brèche de Roland has all but disappeared and care will be needed in descending a combination of snowfield, moraine and possibly small rocksteps, depending on the time of year. The multitudes visiting the col mean that the route is clear and well-trod. Booking is essential at the busy Refuge de la Brèche de Roland. It would be possible to combine Stages 6 and 7.

From **Refugio de Góriz** follow the cairned path roughly WNW. The path is clear except where it climbs rock slabs or rocksteps and leads you through limestone karst to the **Cuello de Millaris** (**1hr 20min**, 2457m, N42°40.468 W000°00.945). The path disappears here but continue WNW down to and across Plana Millaris, a flat plain, and up to **Collado del Descargador** (**1hr 45min**, 2498m, N42°40.704 W000°01.851).

There is a **high-level route** north from here directly to Brèche de Roland, with an exposed section protected by chains. This is a viable alternative in good weather once all the snow has melted.

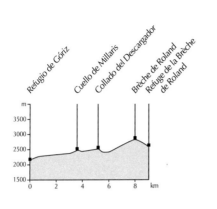

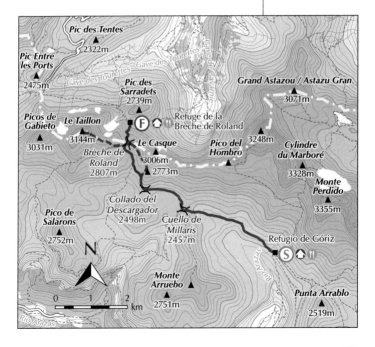

Brèche de Roland

Again, the path is vague, but descend WNW into Plano de Narciso. Follow the right-hand edge of the plain (good campsites), pass a reliable spring and immediately afterwards climb right from a small stone enclosure (**1hr 55min**, N42°40.855 W000°02.192). Pick up an inadequately cairned 'path' and follow this up limestone karst, scree and boulderfield to reach the dramatic **Brèche de Roland** (**3hr 5min**, 2807m, N42°41.461 W000°02.043).

> **Le Taillon** (3144m), to the west, is possibly the easiest 3000m peak in the Pyrenees and can be reached by following a well-trod path to Le Doigt de la Fausse Brêche, a cleft in the wall bordered by a rock pillar. Pass through the cleft to the northern side and follow the ridge up to the summit. Return by the same route.

From the Brèche, initially descend left and follow a well-trod route down snowfields, scree and possibly small rocksteps to reach the **Refuge de la Brèche de Roland** (**3hr 30min**, 2587m, N42°41.761

W000°02.043) which has recently been expanded and fully renovated.

FACILITIES FOR STAGE 6

Refuge de la Brèche de Roland: tel (33) 0683 38 13 24 http://refugebreche deroland.ffcam.fr

---

STAGE 7
*Refuge de la Brèche de Roland to
Refugio de Bujaruelo*

Start	Refuge de la Brèche de Roland
Distance	10km
Total ascent	50m
Total descent	1300m
Time	3hr
High points	Col des Sarradets (2584m)

This short stage, which is a long descent to the Refugio de Bujaruelo, could be combined with Stage 6.

From the **Refuge de la Brèche de Roland**, contour northwest to the **Col des Sarradets** (**10min**, 2584m) and descend below the remnants of the Glacier du Taillon. Care is needed as you cross the outflow from the glacier to reach a junction (**25min**). Turn left, signed for Port de Boucharo, and continue to the **Port de Boucharo** (**1hr**, 2270m, N42°42.236 W000°03.857).

Follow a clear path west, with red/white waymarking. Cross a stream (**1hr 30min**, 1990m), possibly the only water on the descent. Continue down and cross the dry streambed immediately before a cabin which could be used for an emergency bivouac. The descent continues

135

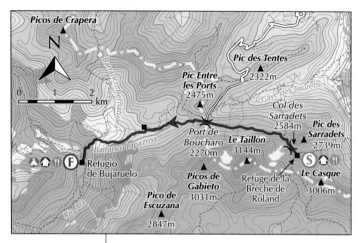

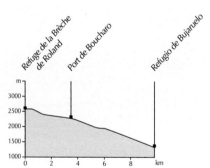

well left of the 'stream' and then drops steeply through forest to arrive at Puente de Bujaruelo. Cross the bridge to the **Refugio de Bujaruelo** (**3hr**, 1338m, N42°41.634 W000°06.469) with campground, car park and swimming hole.

FACILITIES FOR STAGE 7

Refugio de Bujaruelo: tel (34) 974 486 412 www.refugiodebujaruelo.com

---

STAGE 8

*Refugio de Bujaruelo to
Baños de Panticosa*

Start	Refugio de Bujaruelo
Distance	24km
Total ascent	1300m
Total descent	1000m
Time	7hr 40min
High points	Cuello alt del Brazato (2564m)

This long stage follows the GR11 with red/white waymarking supplemented by cairns. The crossing of the Cuello alt del Brazato is relatively easy for a high alpine pass, but there is boulderfield to cross and the Rio Ara could be difficult to cross in snowmelt.

From **Refugio de Bujaruelo**, cross the bridge (Puente de Bujaruelo) and follow the path up the right-hand bank of the Río Ara through meadows then turn sharp right along a dirt road (**25min**). Pass below a waterfall (**1hr**) and reach the **Refugio de Ordiso**, a bothy, at the road-head (**1hr 15min**). Take the path to the right of the bothy and reach another bothy, **Refugio de Labaza** (**2hr 35min**, 1780m, N42°44.913 W000°09.154).

The path stays on the right side of the right-hand valley as the main valley forks. There is a bridge across the main stream which you could use if the river is running high (and then continue up the pathless left-hand bank) but the GR11 continues up the right bank. Just before a stream junction, cross the stream (**3hr 30min**, 1990m, N42°45.947 W000°10.231). It is easier to cross a little below the cairned crossing point.

Climb a faint path to the left of the stream in the side-valley (if you lose the path, follow the stream) and reach a grassy plateau with good campsites (**4hr 10min**). Leave

Meadows above the Puente de Bujaruelo

this to the left of the right-hand stream and climb boulderfield to the right of a small tarn (**4hr 45min**) and two more tarns; the third is best for a chilly swim. Then climb easily to the **Cuello alt del Brazato** (**5hr 35min**, 2564m, N42°45.483 W000°12.117).

Traverse boulderfields to the west ridge of Punta Bazias (**5hr 55min**, 2510m, N42°45.304 W000°12.445) and then descend a steep, rough path to the northwest end of the Embalse del Brazato **reservoir** (**6hr 15min**, 2384m, N42°45.157 W000°12.759).

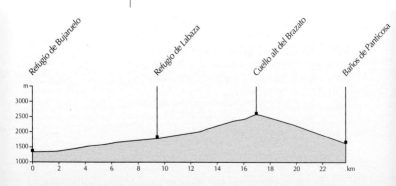

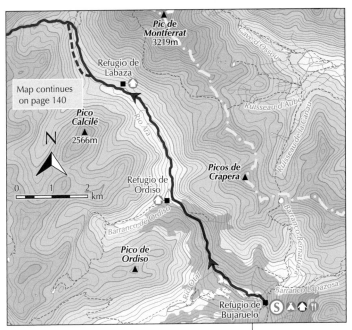

Map continues on page 140

Head roughly north and veer left as you descend down a rough path to a pipeline (**6hr 35min**). There are campsites, probably with water about 200 metres to the left. Head diagonally left below the pipeline and follow a good path which switchbacks down to **Baños de Panticosa**. Descend steps then keep straight on to reach the Refugio Casa de Piedra at the far right end of the resort (**7hr 40min**, 1636m, N42°45.811 W000°14.050).

Baños de Panticosa is a 'thermal spa' resort catering for those with big budgets. Fortunately, there is a refuge, Refugio Casa de Piedra, which is open all year, as well as the five-star Gran Hotel (with casino) and the four-star Hotel Continental. There is also a café, bar and restaurant, but only a souvenir shop.

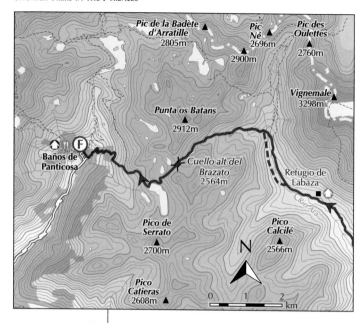

STAGE 9

Baños de Panticosa to Refugio de Respomuso

Start	Baños de Panticosa
Distance	17km
Total ascent	1300m
Total descent	700m
Time	6hr 40min
High points	Cuello de l'Infierno (2721m), Cuello de Tebarrai (2781m)
Warning	The descent from Cuello de Tebarrai is extremely steep; ice-axe and crampons are required prior to snowmelt.

This stage follows the GR11 with red/white waymarking supplemented by cairns. It is a rough, tough stage with a crossing of high passes in the Picos del Infierno. The descent of an uncomfortably steep gully from the Cuello de Tebarrai is possibly the most difficult on the GR11, especially when snow-covered in early season. In snow, alpine gear would be required for a safe descent.

In **Baños de Panticosa**, follow the path to the right of Refugio Casa de Piedra, climbing left of the cascading Río Caldarés. After 45min pass good campsites, with

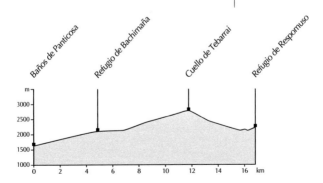

141

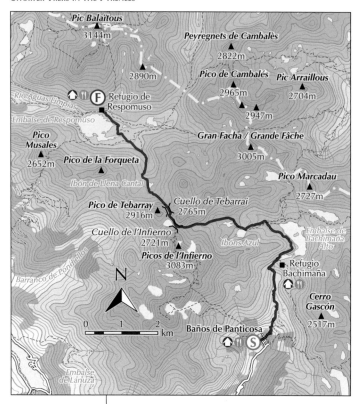

waterholes in the stream and continue up to a junction by a small dam (**1hr 50min**, 2180m, N42°46.840 W000°13.757). **Refugio de Bachimaña** is on the knoll across the dam.

The GR11 continues above the left shore of the Embalse de Bachimaña Bajo and the larger **Embalse de Bachimaña Alto** to cross the main stream on stepping-stones and reach a signpost (**2hr 35min**, 2201m, N42°47.373 W000°13.970). Head east, signed to Refugio de Respomuso, and follow the path to Ibón Azul Inferior and continue well right of this lake to Ibón Azul

Superior with the last good campsites on the ascent (**3hr 25min**, 2445m, N42°47.451 W000°14.793). Follow an often faint but well-waymarked path up the valley, predominantly over boulderfield which could hold significant snowfields well into summer, to arrive at the **Cuello de l'Infierno** (**4hr 35min**, 2721m, N42°47.357 W000°15.858).

Contour right along a path across the scree slope to a short easy scramble to the **Cuello de Tebarrai** (Collado de Piedrafita) (**4hr 50min**, 2781m, N42°47.525 W000°16.006). Now descend a nasty gully (in snow, ice-axe and crampons are required for a safe descent) before gradually veering left through easier scree and boulderfield.

Arrive at **Ibón de Llena Cantal**, where camping and a chilly swim are possible (**5hr 30min**, 2430m, N42°48.011 W000°16.443). Continue down the GR11, crossing and recrossing the stream, and go down to the main path round the south side of the **Embalse de Respomuso**. Turn left and soon fork right and cross the streams feeding the southeast tip of the reservoir, possibly getting wet feet (**6hr 10min**, 2120m, N42°48.721 W000°16.998).

Pico Llena Cantal over Refugio de Respomuso

Go half-left and climb over the spur to reach the northeast tip of the reservoir and continue left to the **Refugio de Respomuso** (**6hr 40min**, 2208m, N42°49.009 W000°17.268). Camping is not permitted at the refuge, but there are plenty of good sites on the approach. The refuge is a base for climbs on the south side of Balaïtous (3144m).

FACILITIES FOR STAGE 9

Bachimaña

Refugio de Bachimaña: tel (34) 697 126 967 www.alberguesyrefugiosdearagon.com

End of stage

Refugio de Respomuso: tel (34) 974 337 556 www.alberguesyrefugiosdearagon.com

STAGE 10
Refugio de Respomuso to Refuge Wallon

Start	Refugio de Respomuso
Distance	12km
Total ascent	600m
Total descent	1000m
Time	4hr 25min
High points	Col de Fache (2664m)

There is no waymarking on this stage, which follows cairned paths. The proliferation of cairns en route to the Col de Fache could make navigation difficult in mist when crossing the boulderfields or in early season with snowfields. Col de Fache is relatively easy for a high pass and leads to the picturesque Marcadau valley.

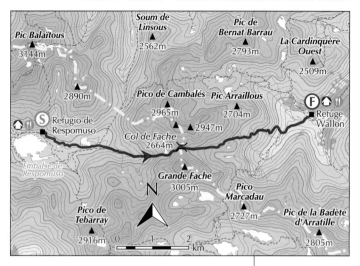

From **Refugio de Respomuso** return to the northeast tip of the reservoir, then fork left off the GR11, pass two tarns, Ibónes de las Ranas (swimming possible), and reach a massive dam to a reservoir which was never completed. Follow the path to the left of the dam wall and cross the outlet to the Ibón de Campoplano (**40min**, 2140m,

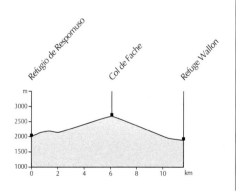

145

Refuge Wallon

The climb of the Grande Fache (3005m) to the south is graded F and the ascent is described as an easy scramble.

N42°48.839 W000°16.189) with the last comfortable camping until well down the descent.

Head east and follow the path up the right-hand side of the cascading stream to the 'false col' and the Ibones de la Faixa (**2hr 10min**, 2520m, N42°48.711 W000°14.696). Continue up rougher paths and boulder-field, to the right of the lakes, to reach the **Col de Fache** (**2hr 45min**, 2664m, N42°48.765 W000°14.338). ◀

The descent path is to the left of the col, to avoid boulderfields and snowfields, and descends gently down the southern slopes of Petite Fache, not down the valley. After passing well left of a tarn, descend a side-valley, passing a small tarn (2290m) where swimming is possible, and then follow a good switchbacking path to reach a junction by a bridge in the Macadau valley (**4hr 10min**, 1940m, N42°48.966 W000°12.253).

Cross the bridge and follow the path down, then recross the river. There is a swimming hole under the bridge, the aire de bivouac is on your left and **Refuge Wallon** is straight ahead (**4hr 25min**, 1865m, N42°49.200 W000°11.689).

FACILITIES FOR STAGE 10

Refuge Wallon: tel (33) 0988 77 37 90 www.refuge-marcadau.csvss.fr

STAGE 11
Refuge Wallon to Cauterets

Start	Refuge Wallon
Distance	21km
Total ascent	800m
Total descent	1700m
Time	6hr 45min
High points	Lac du Pourtet (2420m), Col de la Haugade (2378m)

Stage 11 follows a rough but spectacular route over the Col de la Haugade to the Refuge d'Ilhéou before an easy descent to Cauterets along the GR10. There are plenty of campsites on the ascent to Lac Nére, after which they are few and far between. In bad weather or if you are short of time or don't want to descend to Cauterets you could continue down the valley to Pont d'Espagne – see alternative description. From Pont d'Espagne you could either continue to Cauterets or head up to Refuge des Oulettes de Gaube as described in Stage 1.

From **Refuge Wallon** take the path northwest, signed to Lac Nére, and continue to a signed junction by the second small stream (**30min**, 2050m, N42°49.564 W000°12.082). Keep right and follow the clear path to **Lac Nére** (**1hr 25min**, 2310m, N42°50.011 W000°12.189), where swimming is possible. Go round the right-hand side of the lake and follow the path north to **Lac du Pourtet**. Continue round the right-hand side of this lake until about 50 metres before the outlet stream (**2hr 5min**, 2420m N42°50.583 W000°12.097) and

Lac Nére

descend east on the switchbacking path, past a tarn to a signed path junction (**2hr 43min**, 2220m, N42°50.635 W000°11.436) just before a small stream.

The main path descends right to Pont d'Espagne but instead follow the faint rough cairned path (with an assortment of old waymarks), often over boulderfield, which rises gradually. Ignore a descending path right and

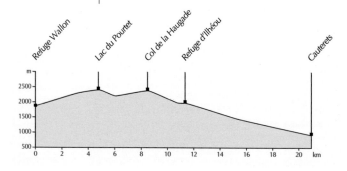

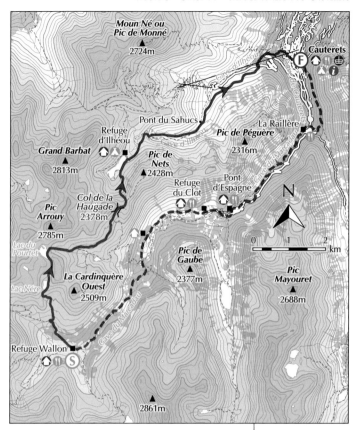

an ascending path left to reach the **Col de la Haugade** (**3hr 45min**, 2378m, N42°51.223 W000°10.507).

Descend left to a second col (2311m), with good but exposed campsites, and descend the clear path to the aire de bivouac (**4hr 30min**) beside the Lac d'Ilhéou. ▸ Turn right to the **Refuge d'Ilhéou** at the northeast tip of the lake (**4hr 40min**, 1988m, N42°51.967 W000°10.143).

Now follow the GR10, with good red/white way-marking, to Cauterets. Initially it is easier to descend

Swimming is possible from the bivouac area.

149

the track than follow the GR10 which shortcuts the switchbacks in the track. When you reach the **Pont de Sahucs**, with information boards (**5hr 25min**, 1480m, N42°52.387 W000°08.876), leave the track and follow the GR10 down the right-hand side of the stream. Fork left to stay beside the stream and then roughly contour before descending alongside a wall and along a walled path to reach a road by a farm (**6hr 10min**, 1290m, N42°53.260 W000°07.565) with water point.

Turn left, then fork right down a track into the woods. Turn sharp right under the ski lift, then sharp left down a path and switchback down to regain the road. Descend right then keep straight on down a path at the next sharp bend. Turn left at a junction and then descend a flood defence wall into **Cauterets**. Turn right and left to reach the tourist office, with public toilets, in the town centre (**6hr 45min**, 925m, N42°53.323 W000°06.869).

Alternative: Refuge Wallon to Cauterets via Pont d'Espagne

From the refuge, continue down the left side of the valley, eventually crossing the river (**40min**). Further down, either follow the track or short-cut left along a path to arrive at Plateau de Clot. Cross the river on a bridge to the left (**1hr 5min**) and follow the track down the left-hand side of the valley, passing a basic bothy (N42°50.796 W000°10.028) before arriving at the **Refuge du Clot** (**1hr 45min**) and continuing on to the **Pont d'Espagne** (**1hr 50min**). From here you can descend 11km to **Cauterets** in reverse of the route described in Stage 1 or climb the path (11km, 3hr 30min) to the Refuge des Oulettes de Gaube, also described in Stage 1.

FACILITIES FOR STAGE 11

Lac d'Ilhéou

Refuge d'Ilhéou: tel (33) 06 85 66 55 96 www.refuge-ilheou.csvss.fr

Pont d'Espagne and Cauterets

See Stage 1.

ROUTE 4

*Réserve Naturelle
de Néouvielle*

Start/finish	Barèges
Distance	70km
Total ascent/descent	3900m
Time	4 stages (21hr)

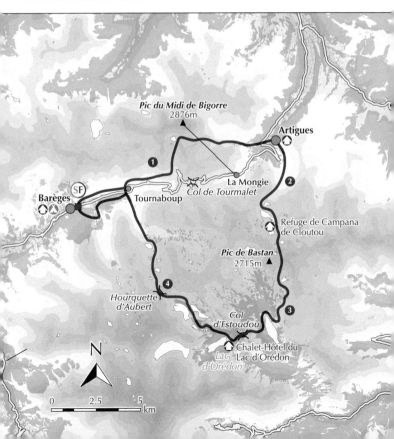

This short trek takes you through the spectacular scenery of the granite massif centred on the Réserve Naturelle de Néouvielle. This is a land of deep alpine valleys and rocky peaks, but it is the multitude of lakes and tarns that provide the highlights of the trek.

Much of the route is on the GR10 or GR10C on good mountain paths with red/white waymarking.

There are opportunities to climb several peaks on the route, including Pic du Midi de Bigorre (2872m) and Pic de Bastan (2715m). There is also the possibility of staying at other refuges on the route and taking your time to explore these impressive valleys and mountains.

Camping is not allowed in the Réserve Naturelle de Néouvielle except at three designated *aires de bivouac* (at Lac de l'Oule and Lac d'Orédon on Stage 3, and at Lac d'Aubert on Stage 4), but you will find excellent wild campsites outside the reserve.

This route should be feasible from July to September. Late July/August in particular is recommended, to give time for the lakes to warm up for reasonably comfortable swimming.

Access

It would be possible to start the trek at the Tournaboup ski area, saving an hour's walking on Stages 1 and 4. You could also start the trek at Artigues (Stage 2) which has the advantage for those who are camping of resupply in Barèges. Both Barèges and Artigues have bus services connecting with the French railway network at Lourdes, but car access will be a lot more convenient. Access from Spain is possible by car but is not very convenient.

Maps

• IGN Pyrénées Carte no 4, *Bigorre* at 1:50,000 covers all stages

Lac d'Onset

STAGE 1
Barèges to Artigues

Start	Barèges
Distance	20km
Total ascent	1200m
Total descent	1200m
Time	5hr 30min
High points	Col de Sencours (2378m)

This stage follows the GR10C, a variant of the GR10, over the Col de Sencours with good red/white waymarking. The climb of Pic du Midi de Bigorre, the highest peak in the region, is an easy option as it follows a good track all the way from the col to the summit. Today's route is north of the granite massif so the terrain will be very different than that experienced on the other stages of this trek. This is a good stage for those who appreciate wildflowers. You are likely to see a herd of alpaca while crossing the col.

Tourism is the now the only reason for the existence of **Barèges**, so it has all the facilities you would expect of such a resort.

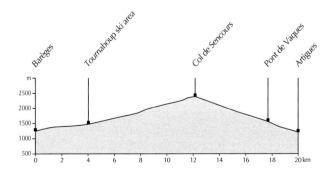

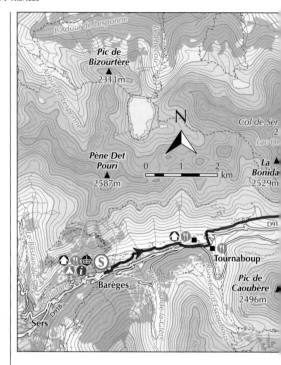

Head up the main road out of **Barèges** and turn left, following GR10 waymarks, across the bridge at the top of the town. Turn right then fork left up a path which immediately switchbacks up to a small tarmac road. Turn right along this and continue along the grass track at the roadhead. This grass track eventually veers left to a junction with a farm track (**25min**, 1370m). Turn right and follow the track, ignoring side-turns, until you fork right to a bridge over the river. Cross, turn left and soon join the **D918**.

Follow this past a paragliding centre with snack-bar, where it may be possible to camp, and the Auberge la Couquelle, a bar-restaurant which offers accommodation. Continue up to the **Tournaboup** ski area with

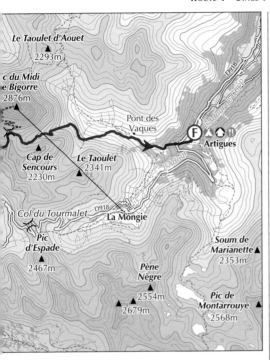

bar-restaurant and toilets (**55min**, 1480m, N42°54.210 E000°06.138).

Leave the GR10 here and follow the GR10C. Initial waymarking in the ski area is unclear so it is easiest to follow the road up to the first switchback from where you can pick up the red/white waymarks on a faint path. This path soon becomes clearer as you follow a rising traverse, gradually veering away from the road. Follow the path until you pass under a ski-tow (**2hr 15min**, 1835m). Follow a ski-piste as it veers left and fork left from this up a faint waymarked path to reach a junction with a better path (the old route of the GR10C) (**2hr 35min**, 1956m, N42°54.823 E000°07.890).

Turn left and switchback right at the next junction for a rising traverse into the Onset valley. Fork left after crossing a stream (**3hr 30min**, 2210m) and soon pass a small lake with the best camping in this stage. Just before reaching **Lac Onset**, climb right up a track to a junction with the main track up Pic du Midi de Bigorre from the Col de Tourmalet.

The crossing of the **Col de Tourmalet** from Barèges to Artigues in the Tour de France cycle race is the most famous Pyrenean col on the tour and you will see many of the hundreds of cyclists who emulate this feat every day in summer.

Runners on the Pic du Midi de Bigorre hill race

Turn left and soon reach the **Col de Sencours** (**3hr 50min**, 2378m, N42°55.851 E000°08.322). It would be possible to bivouac in the remains of the mine buildings at the col.

From here you could join the tourists on the track to the **Pic du Midi de Bigorre** (2876m). This mountain dominates the area and the summit is cluttered with the top station of the Téléphérique du Pic du Midi which takes tourists to the summit from La Mongie, and the Observatoire du Pic du Midi.

From Col de Sencours the GR10C descends into the Coume du Pic. Take care to follow the waymarking in mist as there are many strands and animal tracks in places. At a vague, but waymarked, junction (**4hr 30min**, 1885m, N42°55.947 E000°09.607) the path turns right. Ignore a couple of right forks as you make a descending traverse to the **Pont de Vaques** (**5hr**, 1552m, N42°55.704, E000°10.903). Cross the Arizes stream and descend before recrossing at some farm buildings (1415m).

Now descend steeply through the woods and pass the Cascade d'Arizes before reaching the D918 (1300m). Cross the road and continue down the steep path to a track at the south end of the hamlet of **Artigues**. Turn left for the Auberge des Cascades (**5hr 30min**, 1190m, N42°55.754 E000°12.207) and the municipal campground.

FACILITIES FOR STAGE 1

Barèges (selected accommodation)

Gîte d'étape l'Oasis: tel (33) 0562 92 69 47 www.gite-oasis.fr

Hôtel les Sorbiers: tel (33) 0562 92 86 68 www.lessorbiers.co.uk

Hôtel la Montagne Fleurie: tel (33) 0562 92 68 50 www.montagnefleurie.fr

Camping la Ribère: tel (33) 0562 92 69 01 www.laribere.com

Tourist office: tel (33) 0562 92 16 00 www.grand-tourmalet.com

Tournaboup

Auberge la Couquelle: tel (33) 0562 92 68 15, lacouquelle@wanadoo.fr

Artigues

Auberge des Cascades: tel (33) 0562 91 98 64 https://gite-auberge-les-cascades.fr

STAGE 2
Artigues to Refuge de Campana de Cloutou

Start	Artigues
Distance	10km
Total ascent	1100m
Total descent	100m
Time	3hr 50min
High points	Refuge de Campana de Cloutou (2225m)

This is a short stage and there is a good case for continuing to the Refuge de Bastan in Stage 3. The route now enters the granite massif with the rough, tough and spectacular terrain associated with this rock-type. It continues up the GR10C with good red/white waymarking.

From the Auberge des Cascades in **Artigues,** follow the sign to 'Cascade du Garet, GR10' across a bridge at the south end of the small lake. Pass a picnic site and veer right up a small track, signed 'Refuge CAF Campana', to reach the reception area for the via ferrata in the Garet

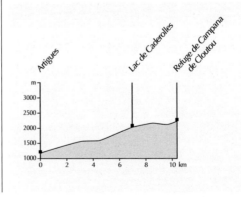

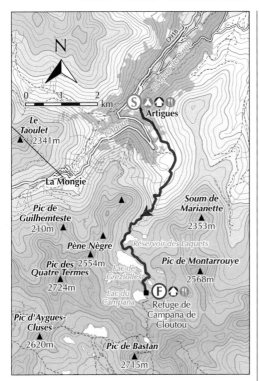

gorge. This is where you rejoin the GR10C, turning left up a small path and soon passing the spectacular Cascade du Garet. Fork left under powerlines and climb away from the stream. Eventually the path levels off in pasture and you return to the stream which is crossed at the second bridge (**1hr 20min**, 1590m). Resume climbing to reach the west end of the **Réservoir des Laquets** (**2hr 25min**, 2041m, N42°53.791 E000°11.993).

The way now enters rougher terrain with lots of crags and boulderfields. Take the path along the north-west shore of the lake and veer left below the dam of the **Lac de Greziolles**. The path climbs above the lake before

The Garet valley

crossing the stream at the southeast end of the lake (**3hr 35min**, 2120m, N42°53.117 E000°12.379).

The path now climbs steeply before veering left to the **Refuge de Campana de Cloutou** (**3hr 50min**, 2225m, N42°52.8893 E000°12.324) sitting above the east shore of Lac Campana.

FACILITIES FOR STAGE 2

Refuge de Campana de Cloutou: tel (33) 0982 12 61 87 www.refugecampana decloutou.ffcam.fr

STAGE 3
Refuge de Campana de Cloutou to Lac d'Orédon

Start	Refuge de Campana de Cloutou
Distance	16km
Total ascent	800m
Total descent	1200m
Time	5hr 10min
High points	Col de Bastan (2481m), Col d'Estoudou (2260m)

This stage takes you through some of the most beautiful terrain in the Pyrenees. There are options to break the stage by staying at the Refuge de Bastan or Refuge-Hotel de l'Oule. It would be possible to climb Pic de Bastan from the Col de Bastan or Soum de Montpelat from the Col d'Estoudou.

When you arrive at Lac de l'Oule you are entering the Réserve Naturelle de Néouvielle and camping is only allowed at the *aires de bivouac* at Lac de l'Oule, Lac d'Orédon and Lac d'Aubert.

Still following the GR10C, head south from **Refuge de Campana de Cloutou**, veering right and left to pass a small lake (**30min**, 2336m). Continue

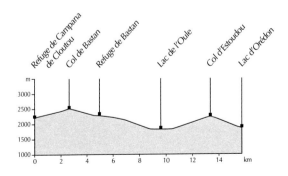

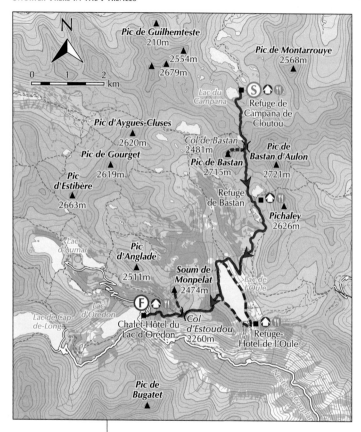

south to a cluster of tarns and keep straight on to reach the Lac de Hourquette (2410m). Keep to the left of this tarn and climb easily to the **Col de Bastan** (**1hr 10min**, 2481m, N42°52.033 E000°12.381).

A cairned route goes right up **Pic de Bastan** (2715m) from here. It is described as being steep in places and, at times, a little exposed, but not too difficult overall.

Descend south to the southwest shore of Lac Superior from where it is about 300 metres to the **Refuge de Bastan** (**1hr 50min**, 2267m, N42°51.194 E000°12.584), a hut in a beautiful setting overlooking the Lacs de Milieu.

Continue SSE, passing two tarns, the Lacs de Bastan, before forking right (**2hr 5min**). Pass left of Lac Inferior and veer left over a small ridge to reach the junction with the GR10 (**2hr 20min**, 2130m, N42°50.557 E000°12.503). Fork right and descend to the track at the north end of **Lac de l'Oule** (**2hr 55min**, 1820m, N42°50.372 E000°11.857). You are now entering the Réserve Naturelle de Néouvielle and you are only permitted to camp at the aire de bivouac a short distance to the left or at the aires de bivouac at Lac d'Orédon or Lac d'Aubert. ▶

Cross the bridge and follow the track along the western shore of the lake. When you reach some information boards and a GR10 signpost (broken in 2018) (**3hr 10min**), turn sharp right and climb steeply up a small path to the **Col d'Estoudou** (**4hr 25min**, 2260m, N42°49.609 E000°11.019).

Pic de Bastan from Lac de Bastan

Turn left if you want the Refuge-Hotel de l'Oule, which is at the south end of the lake. Rejoin the main route via the track along the western shore of Lac de l'Oule.

There is an easy ascent of the **Soum de Montpelat** (2474m) to the right (up and down in 55min).

The right fork is the GR10 which goes directly to Lac d'Aumar, bypassing the Chalet-Hôtel du Lac d'Orédon, the two aires de bivouac and some splendid scenery.

About 200 metres down the descent from the col, the path forks at an unsigned junction by a reliable spring. ◀ Fork left down a good, but unwaymarked, path which descends steeply to reach a road. Turn left and reach the **Chalet-Hôtel du Lac d'Orédon** in 300 metres.

The Chalet-Hôtel du Lac d'Orédon has both hotel and refuge accommodation. The refuge accommodation is at the Refuge du Lac, which you reach by descending the steep switchbacking track from the hotel to the **Lac d'Orédon**. Turn right from the Refuge du Lac to the beach with large car park, tourist office, toilets, water, aire de bivouac (**5hr 10min**, 1856m, N42°49.681 E000°10.135), good swimming and a splendid view.

FACILITIES FOR STAGE 3

Bastan

Refuge de Bastan: tel (33) 0562 98 48 80 http://refugedebastan.fr

Lac de l'Oule

Refuge-Hôtel de l'Oule (open mid June to mid September): tel (33) 0562 98 48 62 www.saintlary-vacances.com/oule

Lac d'Orédon

Chalet-Hôtel du Lac d'Orédon, refuge or hotel accommodation: tel (33) 0623 05 72 60 www.refuge-pyrenees-oredon.com

STAGE 4
Lac d'Orédon to Barèges

Start	Lac d'Orédon
Distance	24km
Total ascent	800m
Total descent	1400m
Time	6hr 10min
High points	Hourquette d'Aubert (2498m)

In this stage you leave the beautiful terrain of the Réserve Naturelle de Néouvielle and descend one of the wilder valleys in the Pyrenees. The paths on the descent are rough but they find the easiest way down this difficult terrain. The path is cairned rather than waymarked and should be easy to follow. It is not terrain where you are likely to want to leave the path!

Take the path from the north end of the car park at **Lac d'Orédon**. This gradually rises above the north shore of the lake before veering right to follow a stream up the

Les Laquettes

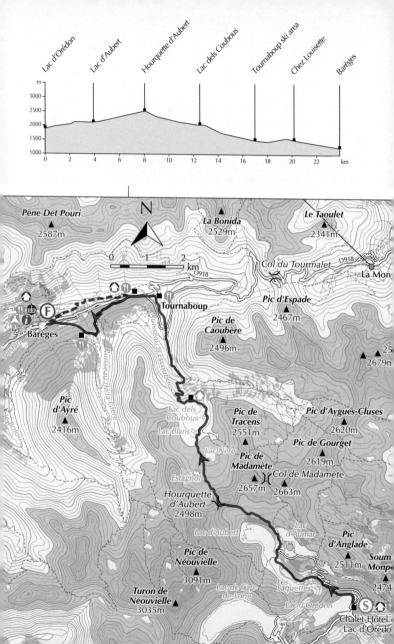

Lac d'Orédon | Lac d'Aubert | Hourquette d'Aubert | Lac dels Coubous | Tournaboup ski area | Chez Louisette | Barèges

Pène Det Pouri
2587m

La Bonida
2529m

Le Taoulet
2341m

Col du Tourmalet

D918

La Mon

Tournaboup

Pic d'Espade
2467m

Pic de
Caoubère
2496m

25
2679n

Pic d'Ayré
2416m

Barèges

Lac dels
Coubous

Lac Blanc

Pic de
Tracens
2551m

Pic d'Aygues-Cluses
2620m

Pic de Gourget
2619m

Lac Nère

Pic de
Madamète
2657m

Col de Madamète
2663m

Lac
Estagnol

Hourquette
d'Aubert
2498m

Lac d'Aubert

Lac
d'Aumar

Pic
d'Anglade
2511m

Soum
Monp
2474

Pic de
Néouvielle
3091m

Lac de Cap-
de-Long

Les
Laquettes

Turon de
Néouvielle
3035m

Lac d'Orédon

Chalet-Hôtel
Lac d'Orédo

wooded hillside. Stay left on two occasions where you approach the road and arrive at **Les Laquettes** (**45min**, 2110m).

Follow the rough path along the northern shore of these pretty lakes and climb to the aire de bivouac which is just below the east end of the **Lac d'Aubert** dam (**1hr 20min**, 2150m, N42°50.354 E000°08.618). Follow the track from the dam to the car park where there are toilets. Take the path from the left-hand side of the car park to reach a fork (**1hr 35min**, 2190m) just below **Lac d'Aumar**.

The onward route will follow the left fork over the Hourquette d'Aubert; however, it is suggested you first fork right, along the GR10, to the northwest end of Lac d'Aumar for a break and good swimming at the beach at the end of the lake. You don't have to retrace your steps afterwards – just head west to rejoin the path. The route then leaves the GR10 (which takes an equally spectacular route over the 2509m Col de Madamète to Barèges). The path is well-maintained and cairned, but not waymarked, and leads easily to the **Hourquette d'Aubert** (**2hr 30min**, 2498m, N42°51.127 E000°07.398).

This is where you leave the Réserve Naturelle de Néouvielle and descend into a wild rocky valley. Fork right before reaching **Lac Estagnol** and pass a couple of small tarns west of **Lac Nère** before arriving at **Lac Blanc** (**3hr 35min**, 2117m, N42°52.202 E000°07.022). This lake provides the best camping on the descent.

The descent continues to the left of some shallow tarns (2090m) and down to the right-hand end of the **Lac dels Coubous** dam (**3hr 55min**, 2041m, N42°52.650 E000°06.966). Cross the dam and continue along the shore to a very basic bothy, then descend a good path which switchbacks down the steep hillside to a junction with the GR10 (**4hr 30min**, 1748m, N42°52.991 E000°06.720). Turn left down the track, again following red/white waymarking, and fork left along a small path. Go straight across the old road, now reserved for cyclists, and down to the **Tournaboup** ski area (see Stage 1 for facilities) (**5hr 5min**, 1480m).

Turn left to reach a road junction in about 900 metres. It would be quickest to follow the ascent route used in Stage 1 by forking right and following the GR10 back to Barèges, but it is suggested that you fork left up the road signed to Auberge du Lienz. Follow this minor road to Chez Louisette, an up-market bar-restaurant (**5hr 35min**, 1500m).

Take the track to the right of the restaurant and switchback very gently down through the woods to Barèges. It should be obvious which track to take at any junction and there is some yellow waymarking as well as waymarking for a snowshoe track in winter. Arrive at Les Thermes de **Barèges** in the centre of town (**6hr 10min**, 1247m, N42°53.833 E000°03.958).

FACILITIES FOR STAGE 4

See Stage 1 for facilities in Barèges and the surrounding area.

Carros de Foc hiker above Estany de Monges

ROUTE 5
Carros de Foc

Start/finish	Refugi dera Restanca
Distance	89km
Total ascent/descent	4700m
Time	7 stages (32hr)

The Carros de Foc (Chariots of Fire) started as a race with the objective of completing a circuit of nine manned refuges in and around the Parc Nacional d'Aigüestortes i Estany de Sant Maurici in 24 hours, and it has now become a popular hut-to-hut tour. You pass through some of the roughest and most spectacular granite terrain in the Pyrenees, with hundreds of lakes and tarns as well as majestic peaks, and it certainly provides some of the most beautiful scenery in the region.

While it may be possible to include a 10th refuge, Refugi Pla de la Font, in the trek, the little-walked section between Refugi Pla de la Font and Refugi d'Amitges would be very difficult in bad weather or for inexperienced walkers, and it has therefore been omitted here. However, on the nine-refuge trek you will still have plenty of boulderfield to cross which can lead to very tiring walking despite the stages being relatively short.

If you stayed at all nine refuges many of the stages would be very short; most walkers will combine some of the stages, taking about 5–7 days for the circuit. If you keep the stages short you will have more time to climb some of the peaks on the route, explore the valleys above the huts or take long breaks at some of the beautiful lakes or tarns.

Camping is not allowed in the national park or in the surrounding area. However, as with the rest of the treks in this guide, times given still assume a camping load is being carried.

The mountain range is south of the watershed in Spain (more accurately in Catalonia) in the central Pyrenees and far enough east to mean that you can expect long spells of sunny weather. As always in the Pyrenees you should be prepared for terrific thunderstorms.

There may be some confusion regarding place names on this route as Spanish maps tend to use Spanish names whereas signs and the Carros de Foc map are increasingly using the Catalan names.

Further details about the route are available at www.carrosdefoc.com/en, and you will find details of the refuges at www.lacentralderefugis.com and central booking at www.refusonline.com, tel (34) 973 641 681. The main tourist office for the area is in Vielha: tel (34) 973 640 110, www.visitvaldaran.com.

Access

This is the most difficult of the featured treks to access by public transport, so use of a car is recommended.

The Carros de Foc doesn't cross any roads but the nearest access is from Espot which is on a minor road off the C147, the road joining Vielha to Llavorsi. From Espot you can take a landrover taxi to Refugi Sant Maurici (Stage 6) or Refugi JM Blanc (Stage 5), or use the national park car park, at Pont de Pierró, between Espot and Sant Maurici and then walk in to join the route (see below). There is a bus link for Espot from Barcelona.

Refugi dera Restanca is suggested as a start point as it is a good option for those who are camping, allowing resupply at Espot halfway through the route. For the Refugi dera Restanca you will have to walk in from a car park accessible up a dirt road from Arties on the C142 between Vielha and Salardú (see below).

Access to Refugi dera Restanca from Arties

Follow the minor road up the right-hand side of the stream from Arties to a parking area by a bridge (1380m, N42°39.479 E000°52.247). Walk or drive up to a second car park with information boards at the head of the public road. Continue up the dirt road, passing a picnic site (**15min**) to a bothy at the roadhead. It is possible to get a taxi to here (tel (34) 629 465 988 or (34) 649 990 515). Turn left immediately after the bothy (**40min**, 1654m, N42°38.109 E000°51.092) and climb steeply through the woods to reach the northwest end of the Estanh dera Restanca dam. Cross the dam to the **Refugi dera Restanca** (**1hr 45min**, 2010m, N42°38.109 E000°51.230). (See map for Stage 1.)

Access to Carros de Foc from Espot

From the top of Espot (1354m N42°34.808 E001°04.967) follow the road towards the national park car park, passing two campgrounds. After 15min fork right along the GR11, cross the Riu Escrita and continue to a signed junction (**50min**, 1630m, N42°35.200 E001°03.208). If you are doing the extra stage including Refugi del Pla de la Font you should turn sharp right here. Most will want to keep straight on along the GR11. Fork left soon after entering the national park. The path from the car park soon joins from the left. Go straight across the landrover track, eventually pass the Font de la Ermita, with water point and small bothy, and soon reach a track junction (**1hr 55min**, 1825m). This is where you join Stage 6, with the Refugi Sant Maurici Ernest Mallafré about 10min to the left and Estany Sant Maurici about 5min to the right. (See map for Stage 6.)

Variations

Experienced mountaineers could extend the route by trekking from Refugi Sant Maurici Ernest Mallafré to Refugi Pla de la Font (around 2hr 30min; tel (34) 619 930 771 www. pladelafont.com) and onward to Refugi d'Amitges (around 8hr). If you want to shorten the trek it would be

Carros de Foc emblem

possible to miss out the Refuge dera Restanca, Refugi de Saboredo or Refugi JM Blanc – but that wouldn't really be doing the Carros de Foc!

Maps
- *Carros de Foc* map and guide published by Editorial Alpina at 1:25,000

STAGE 1

Refugi dera Restanca to
Refugi Joan Ventosa i Calvell

Start	Refugi dera Restanca
Distance	11km
Total ascent	600m
Total descent	400m
Time	3hr 50min
High points	Col de Tumeneia (2604m)

The route was changed in 2018 and if you have an old map/guide it will show the route returning to the Coret de Oelhacrestada (see Stage 7) before heading south to the Refugi Joan Ventosa i Calvell. It is suggested that you take the 'old' route in bad weather when the new route over the Col de Tumeneia, with a considerable amount of boulderfield, could be very demanding. The path was only just developing in 2018 and was faint in places, but the ascent was well waymarked (yellow waymarks), however the descent was only cairned and would have been difficult to follow in bad weather.

From **Refugi dera Restanca**, head along the eastern shore of the Estanh dera Restanca and then veer left and climb to a path junction in a flat area, the Plan de Mar (**20min**). Fork left and follow the stream up a lovely valley. You soon cross the stream and gradually veer right away from it and climb a steep grassy slope, heading for the rockwall of the Serra de Tumeneia. Eventually reach the inevitable boulderfield in a north-facing corrie and continue climbing before veering left to reach the right-hand of three gaps in the rockwall at the grassy **Col de Tumeneia** (**2hr 20min**, 2604m N42°36.825 E000°51.811).

Descend gently left before veering right and descending to a muddy pond (2435m). Climb slightly and veer left before descending to the beach at the west end of the

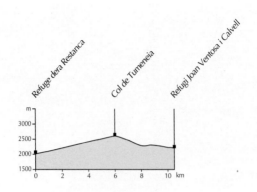

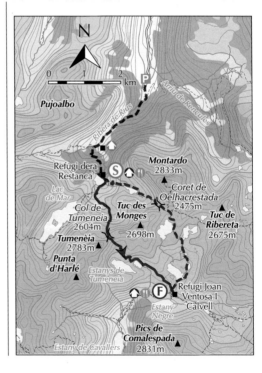

smaller (northeastern) of the **Estanys de Tumeneia** (**3hr 5min**, 2290m, N42°36.825 E000°51.811). Head along the northern shore and follow a vague route, roughly southeast, until you pass between small tarns and reach the outlet of Estany Xic (**3hr 45min**, 2220m) where you join the original route of the Carros de Foc. Veer left and soon reach the **Refugi Joan Ventosa i Calvell** in a spectacular setting overlooking Estany Negre (**3hr 50min**, 2215m, N42°36.319 E000°52.634).

Bad-weather option
From **Refugi dera Restanca** follow the GR11-18, roughly ESE, to Estany de Cap de Pòrt (**40min**, 2230m) and up boulderfield to the **Coret d'Oelhacrestada** (**1hr 35min**, 2475m, N42°37.575 E000°52.528). There is a profusion of paths here, but follow the right-hand path (yellow waymarks), roughly southeast, to the eastern shore of Estany des Monges, past the southwest tip of Estany de Mangades, then cross the outlet stream and fork left at a signpost. Pass Estany Clot, Estany de Travessani and Estany Xic before turning left at a signpost to **Refugi Joan Ventosa i Calvell** (**2hr 50min**).

Refugi dera Restanca across Estanh dera Restanca

FACILITIES FOR STAGE 1

Refugi dera Restanca: tel (34) 608 036 559 www.lacentralderefugis.com/refugios/restanca

Refugi Joan Ventosa i Calvell: tel (34) 973 297 090 www.refugiventosa.com

STAGE 2
*Refugi Joan Ventosa i Calvell to
Refugi d'Estany Llong*

Start	Refugi Joan Ventosa i Calvell
Distance	14km
Total ascent	800m
Total descent	1000m
Time	5hr 30min
High points	Collet de Contraix (2749m)

This spectacular stage is the roughest on the Carros de Foc with long stretches of boulderfield to cross, sometimes with boulders as big as buses, and would be challenging in poor weather. Time taken will depend greatly on the agility of the group. The stage has yellow waymarks supplemented by cairns.

A faint path leads right from here up to Punta Alta de Comalesbienes (3019m).

The stage starts with a rough descent from **Refugi Joan Ventosa i Calvell** ESE to the east end of the small Estany de Colieto (2155m), then an easier ascent to Estany Gran de Colieto. ◀

Continue to follow the yellow waymarks up the valley, soon climbing a boulderfield with massive boulders which bury the stream. The path gets easier for a while as you veer slightly left, away from the stream before returning to the stream which should provide your last water on the

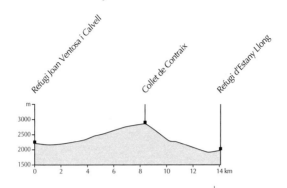

ascent (**1hr 55min**, 2460m). At 2500m you return to big boulderfield along the floor of the valley before the final steeper ascent up boulderfield and scree to the **Collet de Contraix** (**3hr**, 2749m, N42°35.349 E000°54.634). (A GPS reading might suggest a lower height than is shown on the maps.)

Descend scree and then more boulderfield to the south shore of **Estany de Contraix** (**3hr 25min**, 2570m),

Carros de Foc hikers on the ascent to the Collet de Contraix

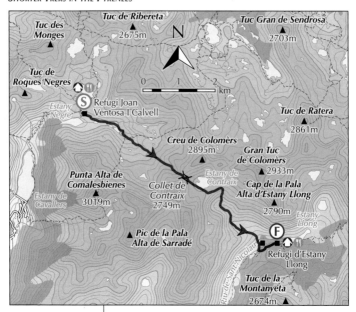

veering round the lake to pass just left of a small weather station (N42°35.165 E000°55.233) before heading east. The path improves but is still a rough mountain path which veers left to clear crags before descending steeply south to a grassy corrie floor (**4hr 15min**, 2310m).

Descend to the right of the Barranc de Contraix to a bridge over the **Riu de Sant Nicolau** in the main valley (**5hr 15min**, 1915m, N42°34.231 E000°56.134). The Refugi de la Centraleta, a bothy, is on your left, but it is only unlocked when the Refugi d'Estany Llong is closed. Head a little downstream then turn left up the 'tourist track' and fork left for the **Refugi d'Estany Llong** (**5hr 30min**, 1987m, N42°34.359 E000°56.540).

FACILITIES FOR STAGE 2

Refugi d'Estany Llong: tel (34) 973 299 545 www.lacentralderefugis.com/refugios/estany-llong

*Refugi d'Estany Llong to
Refugi de la Colomina*

Start	Refugi d'Estany Llong
Distance	14km
Total ascent	800m
Total descent	400m
Time	4hr 50min
High points	Colladeta de Dellui (2577m)

This spectacular stage is made easier by using paths that were constructed at the time of the building of the dams associated with the many reservoirs. The route follows yellow waymarking as far as the Colladeta de Dellui.

From opposite **Refugi d'Estany Llong**, take the good path switchbacking southeast from the main track. Ignore a path off to the left to Estanys de les Corticelles (**35min**) and traverse southwest, then southeast along the western slopes of the Agulles de Dellui. Pass well left of a string of tarns and cross some boulderfield before arriving at the

Estany de Dellui

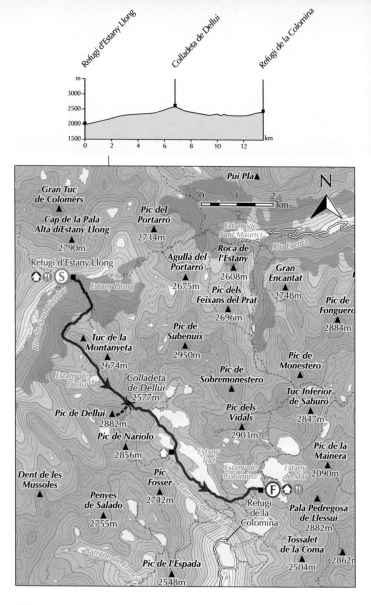

Estany de Dellui (**1hr 55min**, 2346m, N42°32.916 E000°56.941). The lake provides the first water on this stage. Climb easily southeast up the valley to the **Colladeta de Dellui** (**2hr 35min**, 2577m, N42°32.466 E000°57.600). ▶

Waymarking ends here but the path is generally well-defined and cairned where necessary. Descend to the southeast to Estany de l'Elxerola (**3hr**, 2409m) and follow the good path along the southwest shore and then roughly southeast to the dam at the southeast end of Estany de Mariolo (**3hr 30min**). Cross the dam (or cross below it). There is a bothy built under a large boulder, just right of the path, as you start the climb to a low col to the south (N42°31.661 E000°58.500). The path then descends a little before climbing another low col and descending to one of the many dams of the **Estany Tort**.

Cross the dam (or cross below it) and follow the path along, and often well away from, the shore to reach the east tip of the lake (**4hr 15min**). By now you should have joined an old railway line. Keep straight on along the railway and join the GR11-20, with red/white waymarking. Follow the GR11-20 left, soon forking left, away from the railway, and climb a good path to a signpost below the dam of the **Estany de Colomina**. Go right and soon reach **Refugi de la Colomina** (**4hr 50min**, 2420m, N42°31.174 E001°00.068).

Pic de Dellui (2882m) to the right is said to be relatively straightforward.

FACILITIES FOR STAGE 3

Refugi de la Colomina: tel (34) 630 985 321 www.lacentralderefugis.com/ca/refugis/colomina

STAGE 4
Refugi de la Colomina to Refugi JM Blanc

Start	Refugi de la Colomina
Distance	9km
Total ascent	400m
Total descent	500m
Time	3hr 30min
High points	Collada de Saburó (2668m)

This stage follows the GR11-20, with red/white waymarks. It traverses some really wild terrain, which is only made possible by the paths built during the construction of the reservoirs. The stage could easily be combined with Stage 5, ending at Refugi Sant Maurici Ernest Mallafré.

From **Refugi de la Colomina** return to the signpost below the dam and continue along the good path along the northwest shore of the Estany de Colomina. You come out at the north end of the **Estany de Mar** dam and again follow the path above the northwest shore of this reservoir, ignoring a path up a side-valley. The path starts to climb away from the shore then switchbacks to climb a steep

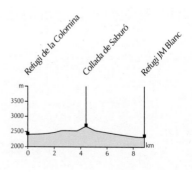

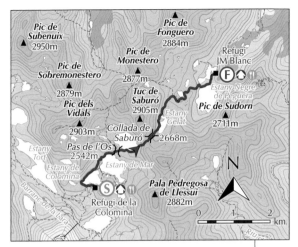

ramp to a notch on the skyline, the **Pas de l'Os** (**45min**, 2542m, N42°31.654 E001°00.650) and soon reach a signpost below the dam of Estany de Saburó. Turn right and follow a 'path' along the southern 'shore' of the 'reservoir'.

Estany Negre de Peguera

This reservoir appears to be an **engineering folly**. All that you see now is a small lake, at least 50m below you, and it doesn't appear to have been full for many years. Before construction of the reservoir the original corrie lake would have filled the corrie as shown on the maps. (The dam is largely irrelevant as it would have only raised the water-level by a few metres.) The original lake must have been drained and an outlet tunnelled from the corrie floor.

When you reach the southeast 'shore', climb roughly northeast, avoiding the worst of the boulderfields, to reach the **Collada de Saburó** (**1hr 45min**, 2668m, N42°31.790 E001°01.270).

From the col, descend relatively easily to pass west of **Estany Gelat** (2527m) and continue down to a signpost (**2hr 45min**, 2440m, N42°32.437 E001°01.822). This is where you return to on Stage 5, and it would be possible to turn left and go directly to Refugi Sant Maurici Ernest Mallafré, missing out the Refugi JM Blanc.

To continue to Refugi JM Blanc, turn right and follow a well-waymarked path which twists and turns, with ups and downs, past several small lakes to the dam of the **Estany Negre de Peguera** (**3hr 15min**). Cross the dam and a few more ups and downs lead you to a track which is followed to the **Refugi JM Blanc**, on a peninsular on the Estany Tort de Peguera (**3hr 30min**, 2318m, N42°32.747 E001°02.656).

It is possible to access the refuge by landrover taxi from Espot. If you want to resupply you can descend the landrover track as far as Estany de Lladres and then follow a good path down the Peguero valley to Espot (about 2hr down and 3hr up).

FACILITIES FOR STAGE 4

Refugi JM Blanc: tel (34) 973 250 108 www.jmblanc.com

Espot

See Stage 5

STAGE 5

Refugi JM Blanc to
Refugi Sant Maurici Ernest Mallafré

Start	Refugi JM Blanc
Distance	12km
Total ascent	500m
Total descent	900m
Time	3hr 35min
High points	Coll de Monestero (2716m)

If you want to avoid the Coll de Monestero in bad weather, it would be possible to follow the landrover track all the way down to the car park at Pont de Pierró (see 'Access to Carros de Foc from Espot' in main route introduction) and then climb easily to the Refugi Sant Maurici Ernest Mallafré.

The Alpina Carros de Foc map shows the route from the refuge going north of the Estany Tort de Peguera. However, this unwaymarked and little-used route is difficult to follow, even in good weather, and it is suggested that you do as most walkers do and return to the junction beyond Estany de la Llastra passed in Stage 4.

From **Refugi JM Blanc**, return up the track to Estany Negre de Peguera and follow the GR11-20 with red/white

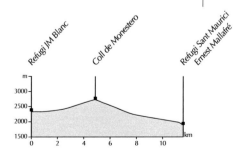

Refugi JM Blanc

waymarks to the main dam. Cross and climb on a path which twists and turns, passing south of the Estany de la Coueta and Estany de la Llastra and right of a small tarn to reach a signpost to the west of the Estany de la Llastra (**55min**, 2440m, N42°32.437 E001°01.822). Turn right, following yellow waymarks along a clear path. Ascend easily, with only a short section of boulderfield, to the **Coll de Monestero** (**1hr 55min**, 2716m, N42°32.612 E001°01.00).

> There is a cairned path up **Pic de Peguera** (2980m) to the left. There is a short scramble at the top which is said to be relatively easy, as long as you find the easiest line.

The initial descent from the col is steeply north-northwest down a rubble slope, after which the way-marked path veers left and crosses a ridge to avoid the

Estany de la Coueta

worst of the boulderfield before continuing the descent. Fork right at a junction with a path descending from the Coll de Peguera, cross a small stream, pass left of the Estany de Monestero and descend the beautiful Monestero valley to reach a track (**3hr 30min**). Turn right and almost immediately fork right and soon reach the **Refugi Sant Maurici Ernest Mallafré** (**3hr 35min**, 1895m, N42°34.726 E001°00.543).

Descent time from here to Espot is about 1hr 30min; reverse the directions given in 'Access to Carros de Foc from Espot'.

FACILITIES FOR STAGE 5

Refugi Sant Maurici Ernest Mallafré: tel (34) 973 250 118 www.lacentralde refugis.com/refugios/ernest-mallafre

Espot

Espot has two small supermarkets and a range of accommodation, campgrounds and bar-restaurants (only a selection is listed below).

Landrover taxis run from the centre of Espot to Estany Sant Maurici, Refugi Sant Maurici Ernest Mallafré, Refugi d'Amitges and Refugi JM Blanc (tel (34) 973 624 105 www.taxisespot.com).

Hotel Roca Blanca: tel (34) 973 624 156 http://hotelrocablanca.com

Els Encantats Hotel: tel (34) 973 624 138 http://hotelencantats.com

Hotel Roya: tel (34) 973 624 040 https://hotelroya.net

Hotel Saurat: tel (34) 973 624 162 www.hotelsaurat.com

Camping Vora Parc has bar-restaurant, minimarket and 'luxury' tents: tel (34) 973 624 108 www.voraparc.com

Camping Solau also operates two *casas rurales* with reasonably priced rooms: tel (34) 973 624 068 www.campingsdelleida.com/en/solau

STAGE 6
Refugi Sant Maurici Ernest Mallafré to Refugi de Saboredo (via Refugi d'Amitges)

Start	Refugi Sant Maurici Ernest Mallafré
Distance	12km
Total ascent	700m
Total descent	300m
Time	4hr 10min
High points	Port de Ratera (2594m)

The two short easy stages from Refugi Sant Maurici Ernest Mallafré to Refugi d'Amitges and Refugi d'Amitges to Refugi de Saboredo have been combined. However, if you decide to add Espot to your trek you will probably want to treat this as two stages. It is possible to follow the GR11 directly from the Port de Ratera to Refugi de Colomèrs (in Stage 7), missing out the Refugi de Saboredo.

From **Refugi Sant Maurici Ernest Mallafré** follow the track down to a track junction (**5min**) with the GR11, which is also the main tourist route from Espot. Turn left to reach the **Estany de Sant Maurici** (**15min**, 1925m, N42°34.932

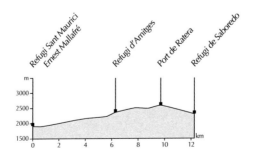

E001°00.591) with toilets, water point, tourist office and landrover taxis.

Follow the path along the north shore of the lake. This 'tourist' path gradually climbs past the Cascades de Ratera to reach the landrover track (**1hr**, 2105m). Turn left, pass the Estany de Ratera and ignore the GR11 going off left before climbing more steeply, passing a water point (2240m) and arriving at the **Refugi d'Amitges** (**1hr 55min**, 2366m, N42°35.797 E000°58.090).

Follow the track WNW from the refuge and, at the track end, continue along the path (yellow waymarks) between the two lakes and climb to a ridge (**2hr 35min**), then roughly contour to a junction with the GR11 (**2hr 55min**). Turn right, following red/white waymarks, to the **Port de Ratera**, passing a national park sign to reach a signpost (**3hr 15min**, 2594m, N42°36.290 E000°57.458). ◄

A waymarked route leads up Pic de Ratera (2862m) to the west (40min up, 25min down).

From the col, the GR11 goes straight on and would take you directly to Refugi de Colomèrs, but instead turn right along the GR211-4. You may find a trickling stream

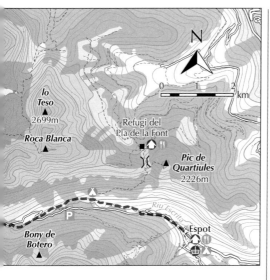

Estany de Sant Maurici

5min down the path and you pass the Estanh de Naut and Estanh deth Miel before arriving at the **Refugi de Saboredo** (**4hr 10min**, 2310m, N42°37.260 E000°57.798).

FACILITIES FOR STAGES 6

Refugi d'Amitges: tel (34) 973 250 109 www.amitges.com

Refugi de Saboredo: tel (34) 661 357 716 www.lacentralderefugis.com/refugios/saboredo

STAGE 7

Refugi de Saboredo to Refugi dera Restanca (via Refugi de Colomèrs)

Start	Refugio de Saboredo
Distance	17km
Total ascent	900m
Total descent	1200m
Time	6hr 15min
High points	Coth de Sendrosa (2451m), Port de Caldes (2572m), southwest ridge, Agulhes deth Pòrt (2521m), Coret de Oelhacrestada (2475m)

There is a good case for splitting this beautiful stage, which passes many lakes and tarns, into two short stages giving plenty of time to climb the Tuc Gran de Sendrosa and Montardo. The going is relatively easy with only limited boulderfield to cross.

There is a faint path up Tuc Gran de Sendrosa (2703m) to the left.

From **Refugi de Saboredo** follow a cairned path WNW down to Estanh de Baish and then veer round the east ridge of Tuc Gran de Sendrosa before an easy climb west to **Coth de Sendrosa** (**55min**, 2451m, N42°37.744 E000°56.829). ◀

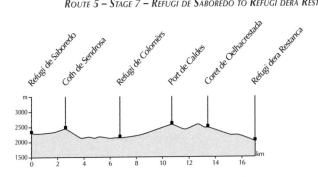

The descent path from the col avoids most, but not all, of the boulderfield and eventually veers left through a flat area with old mine workings (**1hr 35min**, 2120m). At the south end of the workings veer right to climb over a low ridge and down the Estanh Clòto de Baish. Head along the right-hand shore to a path junction (**1hr 50min**, 2146m, N42°37.624 E000°55.855). Fork left and climb, roughly southwest, to a junction with the GR11. You follow red/white waymarking for the remainder of the stage.

Turn right to reach the end of the dam (**2hr 20min**), cross the dam, pass the old derelict refuge and climb left to a signpost (don't be tempted to shortcut along

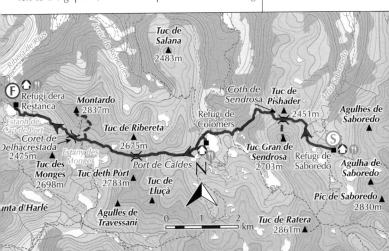

The beautiful Estanh de Cap de Port

the shore). If you don't need the refuge you can continue along the GR11, otherwise turn left to the new **Refugi de Colomèrs** (**2hr 35min**, 2138m, N42°37.449 E000°55.249).

> Don't get confused by the sign to **'Port de Colomèrs'** at the refuge; this is a pass to the south, not the pass you will be taking (to the west) which has alternative names of Port de Caldes and Port de Colomèrs.

Return to the GR11, turn left and soon reach a boulder with signs painted on it. Keep straight on, signed for Port de Caldes GR11-8, ignoring the GR11 which goes off right. Head upstream and eventually (**3hr 5min**, 2230m) veer right, away from the stream, and climb to the **Port de Caldes** (**4hr 15min**, 2572m, N42°37.304 E000°53.735).

Descend left and soon fork right to descend to the outlet of the Estany del Port de Caldes (**4hr 35min**, 2412m, N42°37.405 E000°53.241) and then climb to the ridge ahead (**5hr**, 2521m, N42°37.514 E000°52.939).

Follow yellow waymarks down to an old signpost from where there is an easy optional ascent of Montardo (2837m) to the NNW (45min up, 30min down).

Keep straight on at the next signpost and soon arrive at the **Coret de Oelhacrestada** (**5hr 15min**, 2475m, N42°37.571 E000°52.527). Descend easy boulderfield, pass to the right of the beautiful **Estanh de Cap de Port**, with beach, and descend steeply to **Refugi dera Restanca** (**6hr 15min**, 2010m, N42°38.077 E000°51.279). Descent time from the refuge to the car park is about 1hr 10min.

FACILITIES FOR STAGE 7

Refugi de Colomèrs: tel (34) 973 253 008 www.refugicolomers.com

Refugi dera Restanca: tel (34) 608 036 559 www.lacentralderefugis.com/refugios/restanca

Estanh Clòto de Baish

ROUTE 6

Tour des Montagnes d'Ax and the
Tour des Pérics

Start/finish	Ax-les-Thermes
Distance	125km
Total ascent/descent	6500m
Time	8 stages (41hr)

This trek combines the magnificent Alpine mountains of the Tour des Montagnes d'Ax on either flank of the Vallée de l'Ariège with the Tour des Pérics in the gentler picturesque mountains of the Cerdagne in the French part of Catalonia.

The route is very well waymarked where it follows sections of the GR10, GR7 and Tour du Capcir, but other sections will require navigational skills, especially in bad weather.

There is a website for the Tour des Pérics: www.tour-des-perics.com

Access

Ax-les-Thermes and Mérens-les-Vals are on the railway line between Toulouse and Latour-de-Carol. Although in this guide the route starts at Ax-les-Thermes, those who are wild-camping might prefer to start at Mérens-les-Vals (Stage 7) to take advantage of the supermarkets at Savignac-les-Ormeaux or Ax-les-Thermes for resupply. There are regular trains from Toulouse,

or from Barcelona, as well as a bus service from Toulouse. A possibility for those with a car (you could take a taxi from Ax-les-Thermes) is to start at Les Forges d'Orlu (Stage 2) to reduce the length of the long stage from Orlu to the Refuge d'en Beys. Another alternative starting place is Lac des Bouillouses (Stage 5), and this is also the only road access if you decide to just walk the Tour de Pérics. There is a shuttle bus service to Lac des Bouillouses from a large car park at Pla de Barrès near Mont-Louis in the Cerdagne in July and August, and outside this period you can drive to the lake.

Suggested shorter alternatives

The route is designed so that it can be split and there are three main options for shorter tours:

• Omit Stages 7 and 8 and take the train or bus from Mérens-les-Vals to Ax-les-Thermes
• Stick to the Tour des Montagnes d'Ax by going directly from

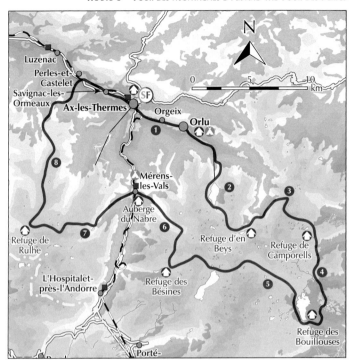

Refuge d'en Beys to Refuge des Bésines, using the GR7 (6 stages)
• Stick to the Tour des Pérics by going from the Refuge des Bésines to Refuge d'en Beys (4 stages)

Maps
• IGN Pyrénées Carte no 8, *Cerdagne-Capcir* at 1:50,000 covers the entire route

STAGE 1
Ax-les-Thermes to Orlu

Start	Ax-les-Thermes
Distance	7km
Total ascent	200m
Total descent	50m
Time	1hr 35min
High points	Orlu (860m)

This short first stage can be undertaken as an afternoon or evening stroll after arrival at Ax-les-Thermes, ahead of the much longer next stage from Orlu to Refuge d'en Beys.

Cross the bridge by the *télécabine* (with water point and toilets) (**720m**, N42°43.133 E001°50.220) in **Ax-les-Thermes**. Climb the steps, following yellow/red waymarks, and follow the road, signed to La Vierge. Climb steeply to the viewpoint with the impressive monument to Notre Dame d'Ax (800m). Start descending then turn left (waymarks were missing in 2017) and left again when you reach the N20. Turn right before you reach the river, fork left along a path, join a minor road and fork right up

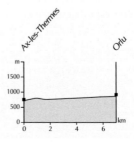

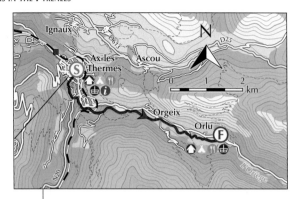

a track. Pass right of the Lac de Campauleil and reach the bridge at **Orgeix** (**1hr 5min**).

Continue up the right-hand bank of L'Oriège with red/white waymarking as you join the GR107. The GR107 soon heads off right and you continue up the river and through the municipal campground to reach the bridge at **Orlu** (**1hr 35min**, 860m, N42°42.078 E001°53.299). Le Relais Montagnard with gîte d'étape accommodation, rooms, bar-restaurant, small épicerie and *depot du pain* is across the bridge and to the right.

FACILITIES FOR STAGE 1

Ax-les-Thermes

Ax-les-Thermes tourist office: (33) 0561 64 60 60 www.pyrenees-ariegeoises.com

Hôtel Le Grillon: tel (33) 0561 64 31 64 www.hotel-le-grillon.com

Hôtel Le P'tit Montagnard: tel (33) 0561 64 22 01 www.leptitmontagnard.fr

Hôtel Le Chalet: tel (33) 0561 64 24 31 https://le-chalet.fr

Orlu

Orlu Municipal campsite: tel (33) 05 61 64 30 09 www.camping-chalets-orlu.com

Le Relais Montagnard: tel (33) 07 84 29 50 61 www.lerelaismontagnard.com

STAGE 2

Orlu to Refuge d'en Beys

Start	Orlu
Distance	22km
Total ascent	1600m
Total descent	500m
Time	8hr 25min
High points	Couillade d'en Beys (2370m)

This long stage, through the Réserve Nationale de Faune d'Orlu, follows the Tour des Montagnes d'Ax for a steep climb to the Etang de Naguille before the crossing of the high alpine pass, Couillade d'en Beys. Waymarking is rather sparse and navigational skills will be required in mist. Campsites are difficult to find on the ascent until you reach the Etang de Naguille. There is a shorter, or bad-weather, option of continuing up the Vallée d l'Oriège from Les Forges d'Orlu and following the GR7 to the Refuge d'en Beys. (The author has not walked this alternative route but is told it is straightforward and well signed.)

From the bridge at **Orlu** continue along the south bank of l'Oriège, following yellow/red waymarks. Pass through an area with giant boulders, popular with climbers, and the Aire d'Accueil des Blocs with parking and picnic area. Just after passing a hydro-electric power station (across the river) you reach a signpost (**50min**, 915m, N42°41.219 E000°54.836).

Across the bridge to your left at **Les Forges d'Orlu** is a large car park, toilets, visitor attractions and two bar-restaurants. If you want to take the shorter (bad weather) route you cross to Les Forges d'Orlu and follow the GR7 upstream to the Refuge d'en Beys. To continue, follow the sign right to Etang de Naguille. A well-engineered path switchbacks up a steep, rocky, wooded slope before crossing a stream. This will provide your first water on the

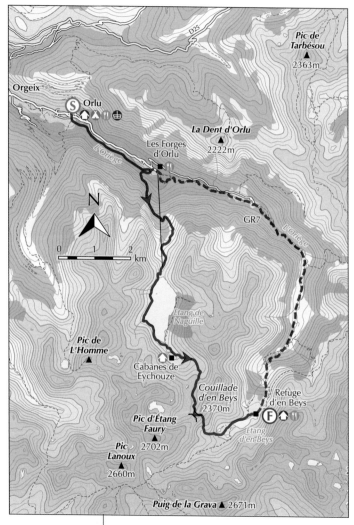

ascent (**2hr 50min**, 1460m). Continue climbing steeply, passing a pipe-fed spring (**3hr 35min**, 1670m) before

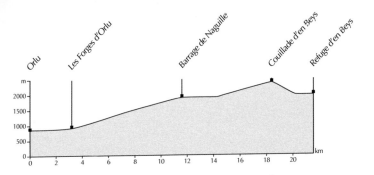

Orlu   Les Forges d'Orlu   Barrage de Naguille   Couillade d'en Beys   Refuge d'en Beys

arriving at the top station of an EDF cable car (1770m). There is a spring-fed pipe to the left of the main building, camping is possible, and bivouacking might be possible in one of the tunnels or abandoned buildings.

Cross the bridge and climb to the right-hand end of the Barrage de Naguille (**4hr 35min**, 1890m, N42°39.674 E001°54.927). Follow the level path to the bridge across the stream at the far end of the

Etang de Naguille

reservoir (**5hr 15min**) and follow the faint path up the left-hand side of the stream. Waymarking is now sparse and is supplemented by cairns. Fork left, away from the stream, just before the **Cabanes de Eychouze**, the smaller of which is a bothy, in good condition in 2016 (N42°38.497 E001°55.185).

Follow the path which takes you left of cliffs before veering right and climbing more steeply (some boulder-field) to a grassy col (**6hr 30min**, 2240m, N42°38.098 E001°55.587). Veer left, climbing a little then descending to the right of a small pond. Contour to the left of a bigger pond and start a rising traverse. Finally, switchback to the **Couillade d'en Beys** (**7hr 15min**, 2370m, 42°37.635 E001°55.572) which is well left of the low point of the pass.

The descent route is easy to follow. You cross a small stream (2090m) before reaching a signpost (**8hr 5min**, 1970m). Turn left, along the GR7 with red/white waymarking, to the **Refuge d'en Beys** (**8hr 25min**, 1970m, N42°37.600 E001°56.648) on the north shore of the Etang d'en Beys.

FACILITIES FOR STAGE 2

Refuge d'en Beys: tel (33) 0561 64 24 24 www.refuge-enbeys.com

STAGE 3
*Refuge d'en Beys to
Refuge de Camporells*

Start	Refuge d'en Beys
Distance	13km
Total ascent	900m
Total descent	600m
Time	4hr 50min
High points	Puig de Terrers (2540m), northeast top Puig de Morters (2605m)

Stage 3 is well waymarked as it follows the Tour des Pérics. There is a transition from the alpine mountains of the High Pyrenees to the gentler and 'tourist-friendly' mountains of the Cerdagne plateau. An early start is recommended to avoid possible afternoon thunderstorms on the Puig de Morters.

From **Refuge d'en Beys** continue along the GR7 to a low col at the head of the Etang d'en Beys. Stay right of a dry leat, then cross it and descend the right-hand side of the valley to a junction. Fork right, signed to Refuge de Camporells, and follow yellow/red waymarks on an undulating traverse. Cross a stream and shortly afterwards pass a small bothy (in excellent condition in 2017) with water point at **Jasse de Delà** (**1hr 10min**, 1960m, N42°38.217 E001°58.105).

Continue the traverse, passing below a shepherds' hut, and a spring (**1hr 40min**) before a rising traverse leads to the grassy **Coll de Terrers** (**3hr**, 2407m,

Vallée d l'Oriège from the approach to Puig de Terrers

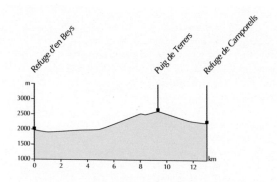

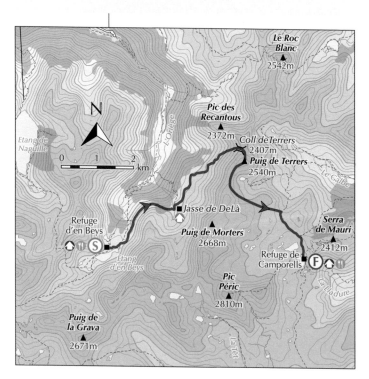

N42°38.996 E001°59.503). Exposed camping would be possible here. Turn right and climb **Puig de Terrers**, with a mountain rescue radio relay on the summit (**3hr 25min**, 2540m, N42°38.794 E001°59.527). Continue along the easy ridge, descending slightly before climbing to the northeast top of Puig de Morters (**3hr 55min**, 2605m, N42°38.245 E001°59.132). The waymarked route actually passes a little left of the summit. ▶

It would be possible to continue along the ridge to the main summit of Puig de Morters (2668m) then descend east to rejoin the main route.

Now follow the well-waymarked route down a grassy plateau, crossing a stream (**4hr 20min**, 2370m), and join the Tour du Capcir (**4hr 25min**). By now the plateau is lightly wooded and dotted with small lakes. Continue following the waymarks to the **Refuge de Camporells**, aire de bivouac, toilets and water point (**4hr 50min**, 2240m, N42°37.317 E002°00.663). Swimming is not allowed in the Estanys de Camporells.

FACILITIES FOR STAGE 3

Refuge de Camporells: There was a change in management over Winter 2018/19 and new contact details were not available at time of going to press.

Estanys de Camporells

STAGE 4
*Refuge de Camporells to
Refuge des Bouillouses*

Start	Refuge des Camporells
Distance	13km
Total ascent	400m
Total descent	600m
Time	3hr 20min

This stage continues along the Tour des Pérics and Tour du Capcir through a 'tourist paradise' with a plateau of sparsely wooded meadows, bare rock and small tarns surrounded by shapely mountains. There are lots of water sources, but this is cow country and surface water should be treated before drinking. This is a short stage and there would be time to climb Puig Peric (2810m) from the refuge or to climb Puig del Pam (2470m) en route. There is a proliferation of paths in this popular area, so take care to follow the correct waymarks.

Puig del Pam (2470m), by the Serra dels Alarbs to the left, is an easy peak (up and down in 70min).

Continue roughly south from **Refuge de Camporells**, following yellow/red waymarks and signs for the Tour de Capcir, passing some small lakes. The undulating path passes through semi-wooded terrain and then crosses a broad grassy ridge (**55min**, 2220m). ◄

Continue down to **La Balmeta**, a bothy in excellent condition in 2017 (**1hr 10min**, 2120m, N42°35.400 E002°00.721). The route ahead is complex with lots of twists and turns, ups and downs, but it is well signed and waymarked. Follow signs for the GRP Tour du Capcir and soon signs for Lac d'Aude, eventually arriving at a signpost above the **Lac d'Aude** (**2hr 15min**, 2150m, N42°34.133 E002°01.368). Turn right, signed 'Lac de Bouillouses (retour PR)', and climb a little before descending to a road (**2hr 50min**, 1920m N42°33.579 E002°01.039).

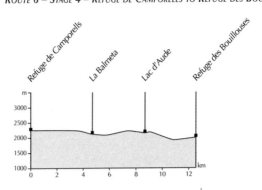

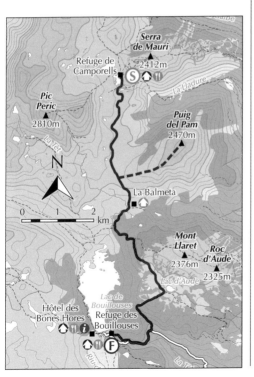

Turn right up the road. You soon pass a bus stop (with buses to Lac de Bouillouses every 15min at peak times in July/August) and continue up the road, then take a path shortcutting right and joining the GR10 to arrive at the **Refuge des Bouillouses** (3hr 20min, 2005m, N42°33.545 E002°00.187).

The **Auberge du Carlit** with accommodation is just up the road, and the tourist office with toilets and water is at the west end the dam, as is the **Hôtel des Bones Hores** which has gîte d'étape as well as hotel accommodation.

FACILITIES FOR STAGE 4

Lac Bouillouses tourist office: tel (33) 04 68 04 24 61

Refuge des Bouillouses: tel (33) 04 68 04 93 88 www.pyrenees-cerdagne.com/en/le-lac-des-bouillouses-english

Auberge du Carlit: tel (33) 04 68 04 22 23 https://lesioux.fr/aubergeducarlit

Hôtel des Bones Hores: tel (33) 04 68 04 24 22 www.boneshores.com

STAGE 5
Refuge des Bouillouses to Refuge des Bésines

Start	Refuge des Bouillouses
Distance	19km
Total ascent	800m
Total descent	700m
Time	6hr 20min
High points	Portella de la Grava (2426m), Coll de Coma d'Anyell (2470m)

The Tour des Pérics follows the GR10 so the route has good red/white waymarking. Camping is possible throughout the route and there are plenty of water sources. There is some boulderfield to cross on the Coll de Coma d'Anyell. Rather than follow the GR10, in good weather it would be possible to follow the HRP over Puig Carlit (2921m) then follow the GR7 to rejoin the GR10 at the Cabane de Rouzet. (The traverse of Puig Carlit does involve some scrambling but it is 30 years since the author walked the route and he cannot give reliable information as to the difficulty.)

Head up the road from **Refuge des Bouillouses** to the Auberge du Carlit. Cross the dam, or pass below it if the gate is locked, to reach the tourist office with toilets and water and the **Hôtel des Bones Hores**. Follow the GR10 up the west shore of Lac de Bouillouses (La Bollasa). If you want to camp, the bivouac rules apply (7pm to 9am).

Keep straight on at a junction at the head of the reservoir (**55min**) and turn left at the next junction for the gentle climb up the left-hand side of the **Coma de la Grava**.

Coma de la Grava

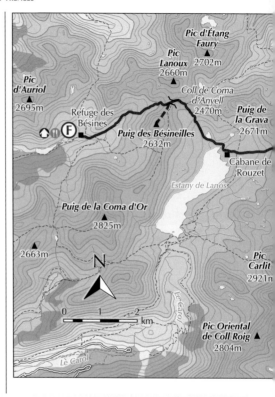

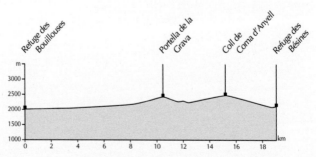

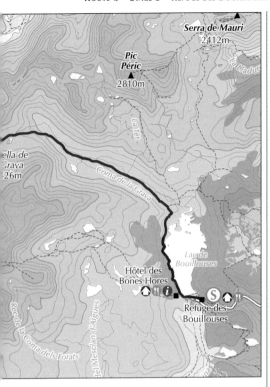

Eventually the gradient steepens slightly (**2hr 15min**); veer a little left and climb to cross the outlet (**2hr 50min**, 2290m, N42°36.069 E001°56.628) from a small lake, L'Estanyol. Pass right of the lake and follow the obvious, but stranded path to the **Portella de la Grava** (**3hr 15min**, 2426m, N42°35.960 E001°56.032).

> **Puig de la Grava** (2671m), to the right, is an easy peak and spectacular viewpoint following a faint cairned path (up and down in 1hr).

From the *portella*, descend the main (ie waymarked) path to the **Cabane de Rouzet** (2260m), which may be available as a bothy when not being used by the herdsman. Climb a little then descend to the inlet stream (**3hr 50min**, 2220m, N42°35.990 E001°54.943) of the Estany de Lanós (Lac Lanoux).

Now head for the Coll de Coma d'Anyell along a sometimes-faint path, passing left of the shallow Estany de Lanoset to reach a signed junction (2450m). Turn left and contour to the **Coll de Coma d'Anyell** (**4hr 55min**, 2470m, N42°36.632 E001°53.889).

> **Puig des Bésineilles** (2632m), to the left, is an easy summit (up and down in 45min). There is an alternative route which skirts left of Puig des Bésineilles to the Portella de Lanós (2530m) before descending west and rejoining the main route before reaching the Refuge des Bésines.

From the col, keep straight on and descend, often over boulderfield. Cross the main stream (2220m) and continue down the right-hand side of the stream to a signpost where the alternative route rejoins (**6hr 5min**, 2110m). Shortly afterwards veer right and climb to the **Refuge des Bésines** (**6hr 10min**, 2104m, N42°36.2283 E001°52.116) which has an aire de bivouac.

FACILITIES FOR STAGE 5

Refuge des Bésines: tel (33) 09 88 77 35 28 https://refugedesbesines.ffcam.fr

STAGE 6

*Refuge des Bésines to Auberge du
Nabre (Mérens-les-Vals)*

Start	Refuge des Bésines
Distance	11km
Total ascent	300m
Total descent	1200m
Time	3hr 30min
High points	Porteille des Bésines (2333m)

Still following the well-waymarked GR10, after a short climb to the Porteille des Bésines the route takes a long descent to Mérens-les-Vals. This is a short stage so there will be plenty of time to soak in the hot springs about 10min above the Auberge du Nabre. The stage ends at the Auberge du Nabre in Le Soula as are no facilities in Mérens-les-Vals, 10 minutes ahead, except for the municipal campground which is 1.3km south of Mérens-les-Vals and has a small épicerie.

From **Refuge des Bésines** follow the GR10 north across complex terrain then veer left and descend a little before veering right and following a clear path up the valley

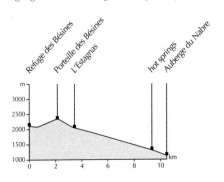

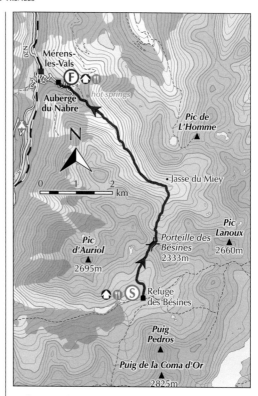

to the **Porteille des Bésines** (**1hr**, 2333m, N42°36.938 E001°52.334).

The descent starts to the right, to avoid the worst of the boulderfield, and takes you down to L'Estagnas (**1hr 35min**, 2040m). Swimming is possible but, being in a north-facing corrie, it is one of the colder tarns. There is a good campsite on a knoll just beyond the tarn.

Continue down to the main valley (**2hr** 1860m) at **Jasse du Miey** and veer left. Cross to the north bank at a bridge (1760m) and shortly afterwards (1745m) pass a waterfall with possible swimming in its rockpool. The path now stays well above the cascading stream and takes you past some pools fed by **hot springs** (**3hr 20min**, 1270m).

Continue down to Vives, the top hamlet above Mérens-les-Vals, and shortcut the road down to the **Auberge du Nabre** (**3hr 30min**, 1135m) with chambres d'hôtes, gîte d'étape and a full meals service.

FACILITIES FOR STAGE 6

L'Auberge du Nabre: tel (33) 0561 01 89 36 www.aubergedunabre.com

Camping Municipal Mérens-les-Vals (with épicerie open 8–10am and 5.30–7.30pm): tel (33) 0561 02 85 40 www.camping.merenslesvals.fr

STAGE 7
*Auberge du Nabre (Mérens-les-Vals) to
Refuge de Rulhe*

Start	Auberge du Nabre
Distance	16km
Total ascent	1600m
Total descent	600m
Time	6hr 15min
High points	Crête de la Lhasse (2439m), Col des Calmettes (2331m)

This stage again follows the GR10 with good waymarking. An early start is recommended to try and beat any late-afternoon thunderstorms on the high passes at the end of the stage. After a long, easy ascent to the Crête de la Lhasse, much of the route is on boulderfield. There is frequent access to water and lots of places to camp.

From **Auberge du Nabre** continue down beside the river to Mérens-les-Vals to reach the busy N20. Turn left and

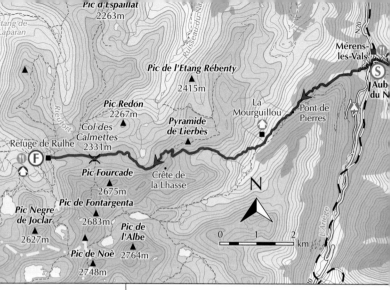

then right over the bridge across L'Ariège (**10min**, 1055m, N42°39.380 E001°50.129) with a water point on the right and the municipal campground 1.3km up the west bank.

Turn left and right and follow red/white waymarks up the left then right side of the Ruisseau du Mourguillou. Pass the **Pont de Pierres**, an old stone bridge, and arrive at the small Mourguillou bothy which was in excellent condition in 2017 (**1hr 50min**, 1660m, N42°38.412 E001°47.904). The bothy is tucked away on the right just

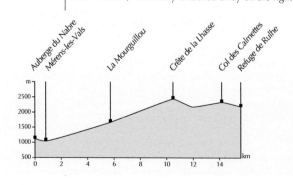

Refuge de Rulhe

before a small pool in the river where swimming is possible. Fork right along a faint path just after the pool and follow it as it climbs to the **Crête de la Lhasse**. When you reach the ridge turn left up it and soon reach a signpost (**4hr 20min**, 2439m, N42°38.272 E001°45.945).

Switchback down, then traverse boulderfield high above Etang Bleu, a typical corrie lake, then climb past an unnamed tarn (with camping for a couple of small tents) and up to the **Col des Calmettes** (**5hr 50min**, 2331m, N42°38.207 E001°44.442). Descend the right side of the valley to the **Refuge de Rulhe** (**6hr 15min**, 2185m, N42°38.279 E001°43.550).

FACILITIES FOR STAGE 7

Refuge du Rulhe: tel (33) 05 61 65 65 01 or (33) 06 74 24 50 71 (when closed)
https://rulhe.com

STAGE 8
*Refuge de Rulhe to
Ax-les-Thermes*

Start	Refuge de Rulhe
Distance	24km
Total ascent	400m
Total descent	1900m
Time	6hr 30min
High points	Col de Terre Negre (2304m), Pic d'Espaillat (2263m)

The route initially follows the well-waymarked GR10 on a magnificent high-level ridge walk, which would be very exposed in a storm. There follows the long descent of the inadequately waymarked Tour des Montagnes d'Ax. Navigational skills will be required, and GPS may be useful. Although there are a lot of streams on the descent many will only be trickling by the end of the summer and they could be badly polluted by the cattle that use the area. There are plenty of places to camp.

From the **Refuge de Rulhe**, follow the GR10, signed to Plateau de Beille, soon turning right at a junction to reach the **Col de Terre Negre** (**20min**, 2304m, N42°38.505 E001°43.932). Descend a little before climbing to the **Col de Belh** (2247m) and up the **Crête des Isards** ridge. After a col the path traverses the west slopes of Pic de Lauzate

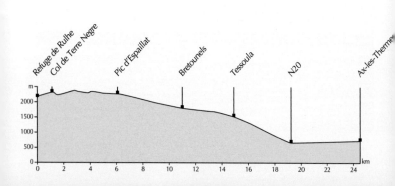

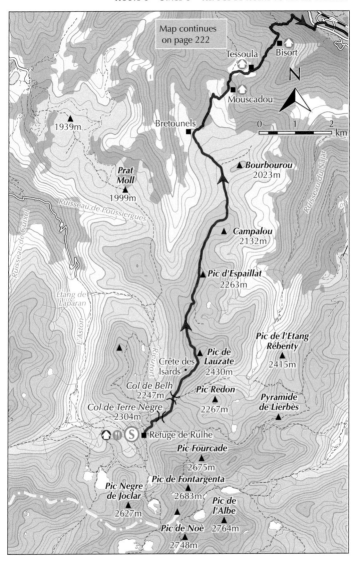

Map continues
on page 222

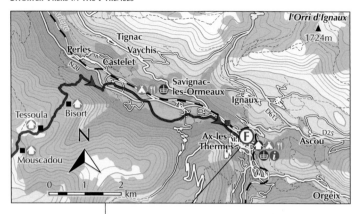

and continues along the ridge to a signpost (**1hr 50min**, 2280m, N42°40.030 E001°44.580).

The GR10 veers left here but instead go straight on, following yellow/red waymarks, over the south top of **Pic d'Espaillat** and on to the north top (**2hr 10min**, 2263m). Continue down the ridge, veering just left of the summit of **Campalou** (2131m) and heading roughly north to reach the col (1970m, N42°41.754 E001°45.466) between Campalou and Bourbourou. Keep straight on as the path contours for a bit before veering left (**3hr**, 1960m, N42°42.138 E001°45.362) and descending through the trees to cross a stream (**3hr 15min**, 1790m, N42°42.662 E001°44.850) by **Bretounels** herdsman's hut.

Veer right (no waymarks) to a shallow col, where waymarking resumes. Roughly contour through the woods then descend gently through pasture to a flat grassy area. Veer right and descend to cross another stream and soon reach the small **Mouscadou** bothy (useable in 2017) (**3hr 50min**, 1702m).

Keep straight on and find the path where it enters the woods. Cross a stream and descend to a col (**4hr 5min**, 1570m). Head roughly east to reach the **Tessoula** bothy (**4hr 15min**, 1530m, N42°43.483 E001°46.011). Veer left into the woods and descend easily to cross a (possibly dry) stream as you reach the **Bisort** bothy (**4hr 35min**,

1274m, N42°43.880 E001°46.620), the best of the three bothies in descent.

Pass the Fount de Coumacourbes (1207m), the only good water on the descent, and continue down a good switchbacking path, and then track, to pass under the N20 at the floor of the valley (**5hr 25min**, 660m, N42°43.110 E001°47.488).

Turn right, following waymarks, past a water point in Le Castelet and past a picnic site as you approach the roundabout for the new Ax-les-Thermes bypass.

Keep left at the roundabout, then follow a track right, along the south bank of L'Ariège to reach a bridge (**6hr**).

> **Savignac-les-Ormeaux** is across the bridge. The Intermarché supermarket, boulangerie, bar-restaurant, snack-bar and Camping la Marmotte are clustered on the old main road at the western end of the village and Camping Malazéou is to the east.

Continue along the south bank into Ax-les-Thermes. Keep going to the bridge (signed 'D82 Centre Ville'), cross and immediately turn right to reach Pont Navette at the foot of the lower station of the télécabine (**6hr 30min**, 715m, N42°43.133 E001°50.220). The centre of **Ax-les-Thermes**, with all the facilities you would expect of a small tourist town, is to the left.

FACILITIES FOR STAGE 8

Le Castelet

Hôtel Le Castelet: tel (33) 0561 64 24 52 www.axhotelcastelet.com

Savignac-les-Ormeaux

Camping la Marmotte: tel (33) 0561 64 24 40 www.camping-lamarmotte.com

Camping Malazéou: tel (33) 0561 64 69 14 www.campingmalazeou.com

Ax-les-Thermes

See Stage 1

ROUTE 7

The icons of Catalonia:
Puigmal and Canigou

Start/finish	Eyne
Distance	224km
Total ascent/descent	11,000m
Time	12 stages (65hr)

The eastern boundary of the High Pyrenees is the high plateau of the Cerdagne. Between the Cerdagne and the Mediterranean is a separate mountain range rising to almost 3000m with rather different characteristics to the rest of the Pyrenees. The valleys and steep mountain sides have an alpine feel to them but the peaks themselves are much gentler in nature, more like the Scottish Highlands, meaning that it is possible for the 'ordinary walker' to hike the summit ridges. The range contains the two most climbed mountains in the Pyrenees; Puigmal and Canigou. Both mountains have a special significance in Catalonia, and that significance has increased as the Catalan people, on both sides of the French/Spanish border, have pressed for greater autonomy. Puigmal (2902m) is the highest mountain in the range, and Canigou (2784m) is the mountain that dominates the eastern end of the Pyrenees.

This route has been designed as a spectacular high-level traverse of the steep slopes of the mountain range with the option of climbing many of the peaks. The route combines sections of the Tour du Canigou, GR10, GR11 and HRP as well as other long-distance paths. Traverses of Puigmal and Canigou are included as separate stages so that you can climb them with a day-pack.

Although you can expect warm sunny weather most of the time, you should be aware that this mountain range, particularly the western end, has a reputation for terrific late-afternoon/evening thunderstorms. Despite rising to almost 3000m, snowmelt is typically about a month ahead of the High Pyrenees; in a low snow year the route should be feasible from May, and from June in a high snow year. In a typical year the route should be feasible from May until October, but not all the accommodation will be open in May or October. These mountains will be very busy and can be very hot in peak holiday season. The month of

June, when the flowers are in bloom and there is plenty of water (very relevant to those who are camping), can make for a particularly good choice.

The main challenge for those who are camping is in resupply, as the tour doesn't pass any shops. The best option is probably to start with sufficient supplies to get you to Chalet de las Conques (Stage 4/5) then to drop down to the supermarket in Prats-de-Mollo and take the waymarked Tour du Vallaspir (on the IGN map) to rejoin the route at Coll de Serre Vernet (Stage 5) en route for Sant Guillem.

Placenames on this trek can be confusing as most geographical features have Catalan, French and Spanish names and there is no consistency as to what is used between the maps, signposts or guidebooks. With the Independence movement in Catalonia gaining momentum (on both sides of the border) there is an increasing tendency to use Catalan on new signposting, but maps will often be in Spanish or French. It's a rapidly changing situation. In this guide, I have tended to use the names and spellings I think are most likely to be recognised.

See www.refugisdeltorb.com/latravessa for more information.

Access
The trek described here start at Eyne, about 5km southeast of Font-Romeu in the French half of the Cerdagne. This is most convenient if you are arriving by car. It is possible to leave the car at the car park 10 minutes into Stage 1. Alternatively, landrover taxis serve the Refuge des Cortalets (Stage 9) from Villefranche, Vernet-les-Bains and Prades: tel (33) 0468 05 99 89 www.canigou-en-4x4.com. By public transport it is easiest to take the train to Latour-de-Carol (from Toulouse) or to Perpignan. There is a good bus service from Perpignan to Latour-de-Carol which passes through Mont-Louis and Col de la Perche. Alternatively, take the Train Jaune mountain railway which runs between Villefranche (on the branch line from Perpignan) to Latour-de-Carol and passes through La Cabanasse and Bolquère. It is less than an hour's walk from Bolquère or Col de la Perche to Eyne or from Mont-Louis or La Cabanasse to Planès (in Stage 12). Another possibility is to start at Prats-de-Mollo (bus service from Perpignan) and take the waymarked Tour du Vallaspir to the Refuge de Saint-Guillem (4hr 30min; Stage 6). If approaching from the Spanish side it would be possible to take a train to Ribes de Freser and then the mountain railway up to Núria (Stage 3).

Shorter variations
This trek can be broken into two shorter treks: a five-stage Tour of Puigmal or an eight-stage Tour of Canigou.

Maps
- IGN Pyrénées Carte no 8, *Cerdagne-Capcir* at 1:50,000 covers Stages 1–3 and 11–12
- IGN Pyrénées Carte no 10, *Canigou* at 1:50,000 covers Stages 4–10

ALTERNATIVE ROUTES

Alternative route 1: five-stage Tour of Puigmal
This is a five-day trek including the ascent of Puigmal. From Eyne walk Stages 1–3 of the full trek, then from the **Refugi de Ull de Ter** follow Stage 4 as far as the junction between GR11-6 and GRT76 (**55min**) above the Vallter 2000 ski centre.
Keep straight on and climb easily to the **Porteille de Mantet (1hr 15min**, 2412m) and descend following occasional red/yellow waymarks. Soon after you reach the L'Alemany stream, you cross it (**45min**, 2155m) and gradually veer away from it. Veer left at a ruin (**2hr**, 1975m) and traverse past a

Stream after Col des Basses in Stage 5

herdsman's cabin and the **Refuge d'Alemany** (a bothy) to a junction with the GR10 (**2hr 15min**, 1965m, N42°27.497 E002°16.927). Turn sharp left here and join Stage 11 for the route to **Refuge du Ras de la Carança** (**5hr 5min**). Complete the trek with Stage 12 of the main route.

Alternative route 2: eight-stage Tour of Canigou
From the **Refugi de Ull de Ter** walk Stages 4–10 of the main trek then go as far as the junction (**1hr 40min**) just before the Refuge d'Alemany in Stage 11. Fork left following red/yellow waymarks, pass the **Refuge d'Alemany** (a bothy) and a herdsman's cabin before veering right at a ruin (**1hr 55min**, 1975m) and start to climb. Cross the L'Alemany stream (**2hr 25min**) and continue climbing easily to the **Porteille de Mantet** (**3hr 5min**, 2412m) with borderstone 511. If you don't need the Refugi de Ull de Ter, you can avoid the long descent by turning left to join Stage 4 at the Porteille de Morens. Otherwise keep straight on (red/white waymarks of the GRT76) and descend to the **Vallter 2000** ski centre (**3hr 25min**, 2166m). Continue down the road to the middle car park then climb right to the **Refugi de Ull de Ter** (**4hr 10min**).

STAGE 1
Eyne to Núria

Start	Eyne
Distance	17km
Total ascent	1100m
Total descent	700m
Time	5hr
High points	Col d'Eyne (Coll d'Eina, Col de Núria) (2683m)

This is a superb start to the trek, climbing the magnificent alpine Vallée d'Eyne before dropping down to the mountain resort of Núria. The HRP follows this route as far as Col d'Eyne and, typically for the HRP, there is no waymarking. There are plenty of possible campsites beside the stream as you climb through the woods and then up the open valley (usual bivouac rules apply) as well as occasional rockpools for a refreshing bathe. The stage is short enough for you to climb a peak from the Col d'Eyne.

Starting from Gîte Cal-Pai (N42°28.408 E002°04.967), head south out of **Eyne** along the GR36, cross the Riu d'Eyna and follow the road until a signed track goes off left. Turn left up the track. There is a large

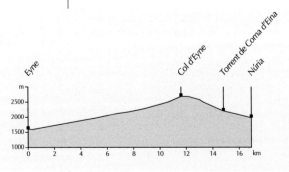

Vallée d'Eyne

grassy car park on the right with toilets and a small information office. ▶ Leave the GR36 here (**10min**) and follow the (inadequately) signed track through the Réserve Naturelle Vallée d'Eyne. Initially you fork right, turn right, turn left and then fork right to get to the path that takes you up the valley. Continue up the right-hand side of the stream until you reach a significant tributary (**2hr 30min**, 2285m, N42°25.729 E002°07.946) where the valley divides.

Cross the tributary and follow the main valley, the **Coma d'Eina**, which veers left. The path gradually veers away from the stream before switchbacking up to the **Col d'Eyne** (Coll d'Eina, Col de Núria), an easy pass (**3hr 40min**, 2683m, N42°25.256 E002°09.005).

From here it would be easy to climb **Pic d'Eina** (2786m) and **Pic de Noufonts** (2861m) to the east or **Pic de Núria** (2794m) and **Pic de Finestrelles** (2827m) to the west. It would also be possible to follow the ridge all the way to Puigmal (2910m) and descend from there to Núria.

It should be possible to leave a car here for the duration of your trek.

229

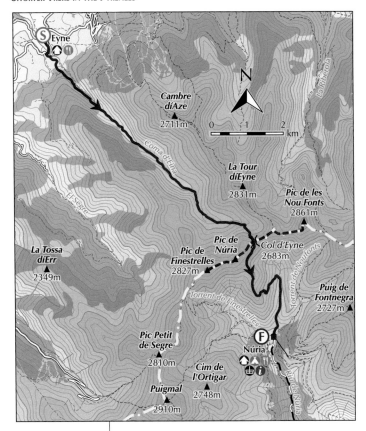

From the pass, do not descend directly but veer right, following red/white waymarks which contour to the SSE ridge of the Pic de Núria and then descend the ridge before veering left off the ridge (2490m) and down to the Torrent de Coma d'Eina (another one!), which is crossed to reach a signpost (**4hr 30min**, N42°24.696 E002°09.488). Turn right and follow the path to the left of the stream down to **Núria** (**5hr**, 1972m, N42°23.871 E002°09.232).

The **Sanctuari de Núria** is a holiday complex with hotel, hostel and basic campground (€8/night in 2018). The shop has minimal food supplies. It is a ski resort in winter and a major tourist attraction in summer with pony trekking, a boating lake, picnic areas, play areas, an excellent interpretive centre, a café and a selection of bar-restaurants. Access is on foot or by the rack railway from Ribes de Freser or Queralbs.

NÚRIA: A PLACE IN HISTORY

According to tradition, Sant Gil arrived in the valley in approximately AD700 and lived there for four years. He crafted an image of the Virgin Mary and later hid it in a cave when forced to flee from Christians. A pilgrim named Amadéu began searching for the image in 1072, after having a prophetic dream. He built a small chapel for pilgrims and found the carving seven years later and the place became known as the Sanctuary of the Virgin of Núria. The wooden Romanesque carving, which is still venerated today, has been dated to about 1200.

It was in Núria that the first Catalan Statute of Autonomy was drafted in 1931 and Núria has become a popular destination for Catalans, especially on their National Day, 11 September. This date commemorates the fall of Barcelona to the Bourbon king on 11 September 1714 which resulted in the incorporation of Catalonia into Castille in 1716.

FACILITIES FOR STAGE 1

Eyne

Gîte Cal-Pai and Gîte du Presbytere (Gîte Cal-Pai provides the meals for Gîte du Presbytere): tel (33) 0608 82 00 99 www.gite-calpai.com

Núria

Hotel Vall de Núria: tel (34) 972 732 030 www.valldenuria.cat

Hostel Núria (Alberg Pic de l'Àliga) is a short walk or cable-car journey above Núria: tel (34) 972 732 048

Núria tourist office: tel (34) 972 732 020 www.valldenuria.cat

STAGE 2
Traverse of Puigmal

Start/finish	Núria
Distance	19km
Total ascent	1300m
Total descent	1300m
Time	5hr 50min
High points	Puigmal de Segra (2842m), Puigmal (2910m)
Note	Times assume you are completing this traverse of Puigmal with a day-pack.

The traverse is much more interesting and has gentler gradients than the direct ascent from Núria via the Coma de l'Embut. Set out early as clouds often envelop Puigmal by the afternoon and thunderstorms are common. The highest summit of Puigmal is shown on some maps as Puigmal d'Err but is usually just shown as Puigmal.

Head up past the camping area at the northwest of **Núria**, cross the bridge and head up the left-hand side of **Coma de Finestrelles** to reach a sign (**20min**). You could turn left for the direct ascent of Puigmal, but it is recommended that you keep straight on, staying left of the Coma de

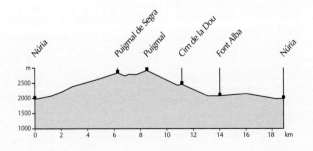

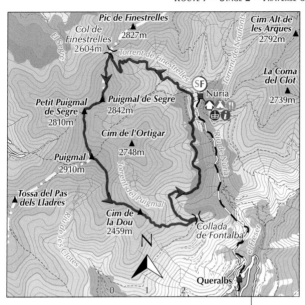

Puigmal

SHORTER TREKS IN THE PYRENEES

Finestrelles with occasional red/white GRT73 way-marks. Eventually cross the stream (2205m), climb over a ridge (2380m) and return to the stream. The path now switchbacks easily to the **Col de Finestrelles** (**1hr 35min**, 2604m, N42°24.511 E002°07.495).

Turn left and follow the cairned path with occasional yellow waymarks over Puigmal de Segra (**2hr 10min**, 2842m, N42°23.825 E002°07.278). Veer right for a short descent, then veer left over a minor top and skirt right of (or climb) **Petit Puigmal de Segre** (2810m) and climb the final slopes to the summit of **Puigmal** (**3hr 5min**, 2910m, N42°22.997 E002°07.010).

In good weather you don't need to go all the way to the car park but can shortcut down to the GR11-8.

Initially head ESE and follow the clear path which veers right and left down the Serra del Borrut ridge. A short ascent takes you over **Cim de la Dou** (2459m), then continue down to the car park at the **Collada de Fontalba** (**4hr 20min**, 2070m N42°22.012 E002°09.10). ◀

Turn sharp left along the GR11-8 with red/white waymarks, for a traverse to Núria. The traverse starts by contouring immediately below the Font Alba spring then goes up and down as it picks a way along the steep eastern slopes of Puigmal, joining the GR11 shortly before arriving back at **Núria** (**5hr 50min**).

STAGE 3
Núria to Refugi de Ull de Ter (via Refugi de Coma de Vaca)

Start	Núria
Distance	19km
Total ascent	900m
Total descent	700m
Time	5hr 35min
High points	Coll de la Marrana (2529m)

You could follow the GR11 which takes a direct high-level route from Núria to the Refugi de Ull de Ter, but the route described here takes the GR11-7, following the Cami dels Enginyers through the steep cliffs of the Gorges del Freser to reach the Refugi de Coma de Vaca. It then climbs the Coma de Freser, a classic alpine valley, and rejoins the GR11 just below the Coll de la Marrana. There are occasional red/white waymarks. There is very easy but exposed scrambling, and before snowmelt is complete there may be some awkward ribbons of snow-ice in steep gullies to cross.

Take the track behind the station at **Núria**, passing to the right of the first chair-lift station and left of the second. Fork right under the chair-lift and pass 15 sculptures depicting the crucifixion of Christ. There is a signpost (N42°23.542 E002°09.397) by the top sculptures, signed to Cami del Enginyers and Pedrisses. Follow this path, which contours below the Alberg Pic de l'Àliga before crossing a stream, which may be dry, and veering right to reach the **Serrat de Pedrisses** ridge (**50min**, 2102m).

Turn sharp left at the ridge, cross a spring-fed stream (**1hr 20min**) after which the path goes up and down as it follows the Cami dels Enginyers along an unlikely-looking

Coma de Freser

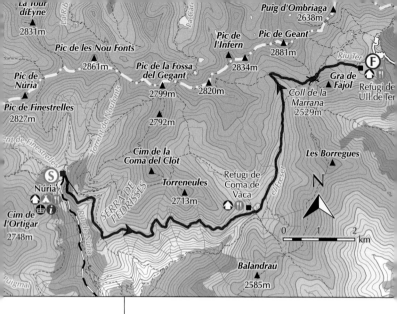

route through the cliffs. While there is nothing difficult, there is exposure and the use of hands will be required. Finally, there is an easy descent to the **Refugi de Coma de Vaca** (**3hr**, 1993m, N42°23.118 E002°13.169).

Cross the river on a footbridge and head up the right-hand side of the Coma de Freser. Eventually (**4hr 30min**, 2365m) cross the stream and climb above it

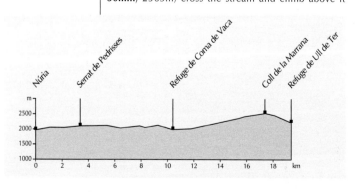

before returning to it at a signpost at the junction with the GR11 (**4hr 40min**, 2430m, N42°25.126 E002°13.654). Turn right along the GR11 to the **Coll de la Marrana** (**5hr 10min**, 2529m, N42°25.034 E002°14.560). ▸

From here you could easily climb Gra de Fajol (2708m) on the right or Pic de Geant (2881m) on the border ridge to the left.

The GR11 now switchbacks down. As the gradient eases (2460m) a faint path forks left. If you don't need the Refugi de Ull de Ter, you could take this path which leads to the top of the ski slopes and then descend a ski piste directly to Vallter 2000 in Stage 4. Otherwise, continue down the GR11 to the **Refugi de Ull de Ter** (**5hr 35min**, 2220m, N42°25.297 E002°15.827).

FACILITIES FOR STAGE 3

Refugi de Coma de Vaca: tel (34) 872 987 098 www.comadevaca.cat

Refugi de Ull de Ter: tel (34) 972 192 004 or (34) 619 514 159 www.ulldeter.net

Catalan ass at Núria

STAGE 4
Refugi de Ull de Ter to
Chalet de las Conques

Start	Refugi de Ull de Ter
Distance	17km
Total ascent	400m
Total descent	1100m
Time	4hr 35min
High points	Porteille de Merens (2381m), Porteille de Rotja (2377m)

After climbing to the Porteille de Merens, the Ronde du Canigó is followed along the high plateau that makes up the border ridge. The path tends to traverse below the peaks but, apart from Les Esquerdes de Rotja, the summits would be easy enough to traverse. Early-season hikers should be aware that the Chalet de las Conques may not open as early in the summer as the other refuges on this trek (the tourist office in Prats-de-Mollo is probably the best source of information on the chalet: tel (33) 0468 39 70 83 www.pratsdemollolapreste.com). If the chalet is closed it will be necessary to follow the track down to La Preste and then the road down to Prats-de-Mollo for accommodation. In this case, it is possible to climb directly from Prats-de-Mollo to Refuge de Saint-Guillem (end of Stage 5) along the Tour du Vallespir (4hr 30min).

It is unlikely that any facilities will be open for hikers.

From the **Refugi de Ull de Ter** follow the GR11 down to the road (2100m) then turn left up the road to the **Vallter 2000** ski centre (**30min**, 2162m). ◄ Take the path (red/white waymarks) that goes up behind the right-hand side of the ski-restaurant and climb to a path junction (**55min**, 2284m). The GRT76 goes straight ahead here and this is the path you will take if you are just doing the five-stage Tour of Puigmal. For the main route, however, turn right along the GR11-6 which leads easily to the **Porteille de Merens**, a broad grassy col (**1hr 15min**, 2381m, N42°25.664 E002°16.555).

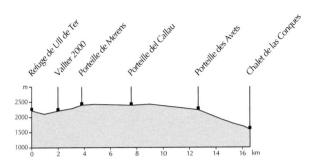

Veer slightly left on a clear path to reach a Mantet nature reserve sign. The eight-stage variation of the Tour of Canigou will rejoin the main route from the left here. This is where you join the Ronde du Canigó, with red/yellow waymarking. Fork right, and veer right then left, as you traverse the Pla de Coma Ermada, a grassy plateau on the northern slopes of Puig de Coma Ermada (2495m). Arrive at another broad col (**1hr 55min**, 2410m, N42°25.909 E002°16.555) on the north ridge of Puig

Camping on Pla de Coma Ermada

239

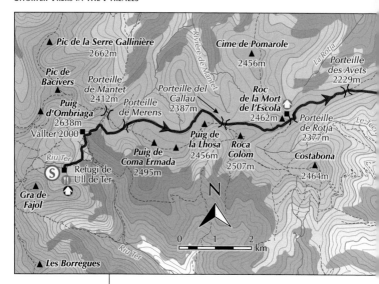

de la Lhosa (2456m). Cross the col and turn right to traverse to the **Porteille del Callau** (**2hr 5min**, 2387m, N42°26.717 E002°18.728).

The path now traverses the northern slopes of Roc Colom (2507m), climbing gently to the next col (**2hr 30min**). Cross the col and follow waymarks, supplemented by cairns, until you pick up the path traversing the southern slopes of Roc de la Mort de l'Escola (2462m) to arrive at the **Porteille de Rotja** (**2hr 55min**, 2377m, N42°25.743 E002°20.249). There is a bothy here which was in poor, but useable, condition in 2018.

Cross the col and follow the path below the rocky ridge of Les Esquerdes de Rotja to reach the **Porteille des Avets** (**3hr 25min**, 2229m, N42°26.251 E002°21.910). This is where you start the descent to the Chalet de las Conques. Cross the col and go diagonally left. The path is rather faint in places, but the waymarks are supplemented with cairns. Cross some streams which are unlikely to run all summer but could be very useful to the early season camper. As you approach a ridge, veer right and descend

Chalet de
las Conques

Cim de
Portavella
▲
1687m

further before entering the wood and veering left to cross the ridge (**4hr**, 1935m, N42°25.867 E002°25.697). Continue to descend, turning right at a large grassy area, cross a small stream and reach a signpost on a broad grassy ridge, Coll Baix (**4hr 25min**, 1693m, N42°25.575 E002°23.580).

Turn left and descend to **Chalet de las Conques** (**4hr 35min**, 1580m, N42°25.575 E002°23.878) with full refuge facilities, but only likely to be open in July/August and weekends in spring and autumn.

FACILITIES FOR STAGE 4

Chalet de las Conques: tel (33) 0411 93 07 33 www.refugi-lesconques.com

Prats-de-Mollo tourist office: tel (33) 0468 39 70 83 www.prats demollolapreste.com

STAGE 5
Chalet de las Conques to Refuge de Saint-Guillem

Start	Chalet de las Conques
Distance	24km
Total ascent	800m
Total descent	1100m
Time	6hr 30min
High points	Col des Basses (1796m), Roc de la Descargue (1980m), Coll de Serre Vernet (1802m)

Red/yellow waymarks of the Tour du Canigó are followed throughout this stage, which is an up-and-down traverse of the steep southeast slopes of the Massif du Canigou, passing through forest and rough open hillside with small alpine pastures.

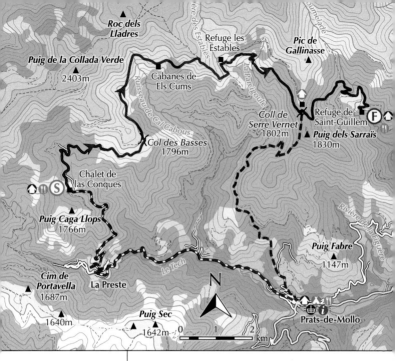

Follow the road north from **Chalet de las Conques**, turning left at the first junction. Cross a stream with a picnic table (**15min**), pass below the private Cabane des Forquets and soon cross another stream with picnic table. You cross several more streams and the road becomes a track by the time you reach the roadhead at the **Col des Basses** (**1hr 5min**, 1796m, N42°26.392 E002°25.396).

From the col you are following signs to Sant-Guillem and for the next two hours you are on an up-and-down traverse of very steep slopes through wooded or open terrain on a path that is very rough in places. You don't need details as all you can do is follow the path. Some streams will probably survive the summer. Eventually you arrive at the **Cabanes de Els Cums** in pasture (**3hr**, 1850m, N42°27.525 E002°525). ◀

These herdsmen's huts may be available for use by hikers when the herdsmen are not in residence.

After you cross the next stream the path improves as you climb steadily to reach a highpoint just after

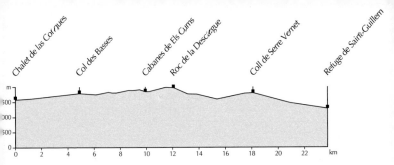

passing the **Roc de la Descargue** (**3hr 40min**, N42°27.572 E002°26.435). (The signpost and French guide give this as 1938m, but the IGN map and a GPS suggest it is nearer 1986m.)

You have now joined the GRT83 and are back to red/white waymarks. Turn right and descend the ridge, then veer left to reach a major track at the **Coll de la Regina** (**4hr**, 1762m, N42°27.459 E002°26.962). Turn left along the track, cross a major stream and arrive at the **Refuge les Estables** (**4hr 10min**, 1759m). Despite its name, this

Orri below Refuge les Estables

bothy is unavailable to hikers from mid May to late October when its use is reserved for the herdsmen.

Take the small path to the right (still the GRT83) and, after 100 metres, turn left down a small track. In a few minutes you pass a traditional *orri* (stone shelter) in excellent condition and useable by hikers who are prepared to rough it. Continue down the increasingly grassy track as it switchbacks down to end at a stream (**4hr 30min**, 1590m, N42°27.708 E002°27.474).

A small path continues across the stream. After about 100 metres, fork left at a signpost. This is where you leave the GRT83 so return to red/yellow waymarks. A generally rising traverse takes us to a ridge; veer left up it before continuing the traverse to reach a signpost on the grassy **Coll de Serre Vernet** (**5hr 20min**, 1802m, N42°27.135 E002°28.497) with good campsites. An old stone shelter about 100 metres north up the ridge ahead could be used in an emergency.

Cross the ridge, veer left and switchback down through the forest, crossing several streams of which a couple may survive the summer. When you arrive at Col Baxo (1473m) keep straight on along the forest road, and then keep straight on at a junction, cross a stream on a bridge and continue to the old church of Saint-Guillem with picnic site and signpost (**6hr 20min**, 1332m). If you don't need the refuge you can turn left here and continue on the next stage, otherwise continue down the forest road to the **Refuge de Saint-Guillem** (**6hr 30min**, 1283m, N42°27.136 E002°29.711) which was rebuilt in 2015.

FACILITIES FOR STAGE 5

Refuge de Saint-Guillem: tel (33) 0978 04 96 85

STAGE 6
Refuge de Saint-Guillem to
Refuge de Batère

Start	Refuge de Saint-Guillem
Distance	22km
Total ascent	1200m
Total descent	1000m
Time	6hr 10min
High points	Coucoulère (1768m), southeast ridge Cincreus (1690m), Refuge de Batère (1460m)

The trek continues along the Tour du Canigó, following red/yellow waymarks as it traverses the steep wooded and rough open southern slopes of the Massif du Canigou. Good campsites are few and far between on this stage.

From the **Refuge de Saint-Guillem** return to the church and follow the path right for a rising traverse to reach Coucoulère (**1hr 20min**, 1768m, N42°27.681 E002°30.243). Turn right and descend gently to the **Col de l'Estagnol** (**1hr 30min**, 1667m, N42°27.838 E002°30.808). Turn left, signed Batère, and contour along

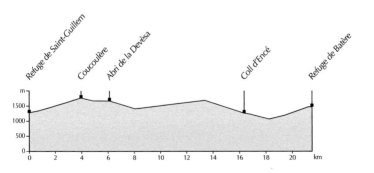

Abri de la Devèsa

Some maps still show the old route which crossed the stream much further upstream.

a track to cross a small stream as you enter pasture (**1hr 45min**). Pass below the **Abri de la Devèsa**, a bothy with water point, in excellent condition in 2018.

A signpost at the far end of the pasture gives you the start of a small path for a descending traverse to reach a path junction (**2hr 15min**, 1420m). Now climb steeply left, eventually crossing a stream (**2hr 40min**, 1480m) and shortly afterwards fork right to a 'new' bridge over the **Riuferrer** (N42°29.058 E002°30.371). ◄

The path soon reaches a roadhead, which you ignore. Instead take the path to the left which climbs to a junction with the old route (**3hr**, 1540m, N42°29.250 E002°30.265).

Turn right and start a generally rising traverse of the steep slopes of Cincreus. Cross quite a few streams, but it is doubtful if any will survive a dry summer. Reach a highpoint (1690m) before starting a switchbacking descent to **Coll d'Encé** (**4hr 35min**, 1263m, N42°28.905 E002°32.365). This used to be a good campsite but in 2018 was covered in beehives.

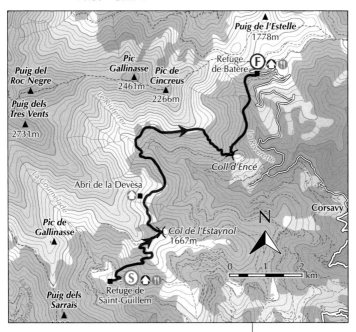

Go through the gate and follow the path left on another descending traverse. Cross a trickling stream and eventually fork left (**5hr**, 1070m, N42°29.548 E002°32.730) as you approach the main stream and start climbing. Fifteen minutes later veer right, cross the stream (1180m) and climb steeply. Eventually veer right and contour to a picnic site and soon reach the road and the **Refuge de Batère** (**6hr 10min**, 1460m, N42°30.102 E002°32.906), whose facilities include a hot tub.

FACILITIES FOR STAGE 6

Refuge de Batère has both chambres d'hôtes and gîte d'étape accommodation: tel (33) 0468 39 12 01 www.refugedebatere.fr

STAGE 7
Refuge de Batère to Refuge des Cortalets

Start	Refuge de Batère
Distance	18km
Total ascent	1100m
Total descent	400m
Time	5hr
High points	Col de la Cicère (1731m), northeast ridge Canigou (2200m)

The Tour du Canigó now coincides with the GR10 and you are back to red/white waymarks. This is mainly a traversing stage along the northern slopes of the Massif du Canigou and of Canigou itself.

From the **Refuge de Batère** switchback up to the roadhead and continue switchbacking up the main track to reach a small concrete building from where a path climbs steeply past ancient mines to the **Col de la Cicère** (**50min**, 1731m, N42°30.392 E002°32.375).

Take the path contouring left and then slowly descending. Cross a stream (**1hr 20min**) and keep descending. Ignore a path right to 'Ancienne Mine de

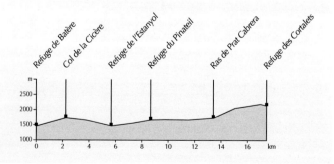

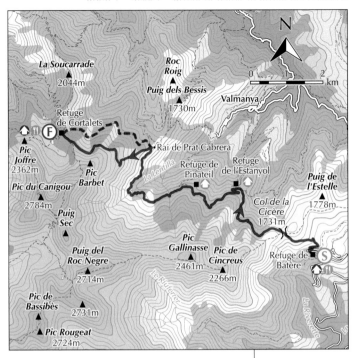

Fer de la Pinouse' and reach a sign at a trackhead. Keep straight on, passing the **Refuge de l'Estanyol** (**1hr 40min**, 1470m), a bothy with water point and picnic table, and climb to pass the **Refuge du Pinateil** (**2hr 25min**, 1663m), another bothy with picnic tables. The water point here will probably be dry. The next 3km is almost flat. Cross three streams at the head of the Lentilla valley (**3hr**) then climb gently to reach a major track at **Ras de Prat Cabrera** (**3hr 30min**, 1739m, N42°31.766 E002°29.761).

The GR10 used to follow this track to the Refuge des Cortalets but that is now considered the bad-weather option since a much more spectacular route has been fully waymarked. Take the path to the left of the track and climb steeply, initially to the right of the fence, but soon

Remains of a crashed aircraft on the approach to the Refuge des Cortalets

through a gate and up to the left of the fence. Eventually the path veers left (for no obvious reason) then veers right to a gate in the fence (**4hr 20min**, 2060m). The path now climbs more gently as it traverses the slope to pass the wreckage of a crashed aircraft (**4hr 50min**). After a short descent the gentle climb resumes to reach a signpost at a path junction (2175m). Keep straight on and soon reach the **Refuge des Cortalets** (**5hr**, 2150m, N42°32.055 E002°27.911). Camping (usual bivouac rules apply) is permitted to the southwest of the refuge.

FACILITIES FOR STAGE 7

Refuge des Cortalets: tel (33) 0468 96 36 19 https://refugedescortalets.ffcam.fr

STAGE 8
Traverse of Canigou

Start/finish	Refuge des Cortalets
Distance	9km
Total ascent	800m
Total descent	800m
Time	3hr 30min
High points	Crête de Barbet (2710m), Canigou (2784m)

On a clear day, Canigou provides one of the best viewpoints in the Pyrenees. The suggested traverse by the Crête de Barbet involves an easy scramble, but it enables a more interesting ascent than the direct climb using the 'tourist route'. Times assume you are walking with a day-pack.

▶ From the **Refuge des Cortalets** return southeast along the new route of the GR10 and soon fork right, signed for Crête de Barbet with yellow waymarks. Climb to and follow the **Crête de Barbet**, often just right of the crest. Cross the ridge (**1hr 20min**, 2710m, N42°31.090 E002°27.837) and descend to the col (2591m) between Canigou and Puig Sec.

See Stage 9 for map.

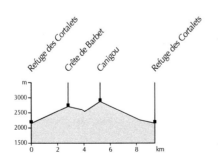

Don't try and shortcut
here as it adds to the
erosion and it can
be a little awkward.

Follow the waymarks down to a signpost at a junction below the col (**1hr 35min**, 2550m, N42°30.804 E002°27.700). ◄ Turn sharp right and follow a rougher path to reach the final wall protecting the summit of Canigou. This looks daunting, but it is an easy scramble, little more than a steep staircase, and it brings you out on the summit of **Canigou** (**2hr 20min**, 2784m, N42°31.143 E002°27.396).

Descend north by the 'tourist route' to a junction with the GR10 (**3hr 15min**, 2260m) and follow it roughly east back to the **Refuge des Cortalets** (**3hr 30min**).

Refuge des Cortalets to Refuge de Marailles

Start	Refuge des Cortalets
Distance	20km
Total ascent	500m
Total descent	1000m
Time	5hr 25min
High points	North ridge Canigou (2260m), Col de la Jasse d'en Vernet (2041m)

This stage follows the GR10 (red/white waymarks) as it traverses the steep wooded and rough open northwest slopes of Canigou. An alternative route would be to traverse Canigou, but it would mean a descent of the scramble down its south face.

From the **Refuge des Cortalets** the GR10 follows the 'tourist path' roughly east to a junction on the north ridge

GR10 west of Refuge des Cortalets

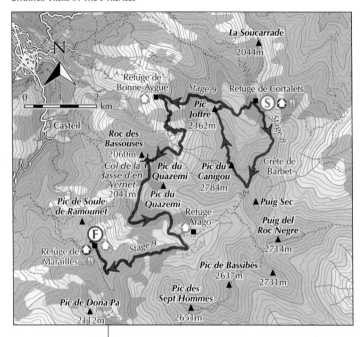

of Canigou (**25min**, 2260m). The Font de Perdrix, marked
on the maps, may be dry as it is tapped to provide water
for the refuge. Fork right for a descending traverse. Pass

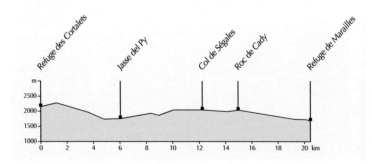

an *orri* (old stone shelter) (**1hr**) which could be used for an emergency bivouac, and eventually reach a track (**1hr 25min**, 1740m). Turn left and soon pass the **Refuge de Bonne-Aygue**, a bothy with a reliable water point and the best campsites on this stage (N42°32.205 E002°26.000).

Leave the track at a switchback (Jasse del Py) (**1hr 40min**, 1750m) and follow a path which finds its way through difficult terrain. Pass the Font de Lescurco (**2hr 15min**), which may be dry, cross the rough terrain of the erosion-scarred 'Les Conques' and climb a better path to the **Col de la Jasse d'en Vernet** on the northwest ridge (**3hr 5min**, 2041m, N42°31.30 E002°25.627) of Pic Quazemi.

Continue more easily to a junction signed Col de Ségales (**3hr 40min**, 2040m), which despite its name isn't on a col. Fork left and cross a small stream before reaching a junction at the Roc de Cady (**4hr 10min**, 2030m). ▶

This is where the traverse of Canigou rejoins the main route and a small bothy, Refuge Arago, is about 1km up the path.

Fork right, cross the Rivière de Cady and pass several more water sources before reaching a picnic area with water point (**5hr 20min**). In a few minutes you reach a col with a car park and a well-maintained bothy. Keep straight on and descend to the **Refuge de Marailles** (**5hr 25min**, 1690m, N42°30.094 E002°24.469).

FACILITIES FOR STAGE 9

Refuge de Mariailles: tel (33) 0468 05 57 99 www.refugedemariailles.fr

STAGE 10
Refuge de Marailles to Mantet

Start	Refuge de Marailles
Distance	20km
Total ascent	900m
Total descent	1100m
Time	4hr 50min
High points	Col de Mantet (1761m)

The route continues along the GR10 with red/white waymarks. The descent from the Refuge de Marailles is complex but it is very well signed and waymarked. A leat (channelled stream) is followed for much of the descent. Good campsites are few and far between on this stage.

Follow the GR10 west from the **Refuge de Marailles** and soon fork right. Pass a ruined *orri* (**35min**), where camping is possible, before arriving at the **Col du Cheval Mort** (1456m). Continue down to the **Col de Jou** with dirt road, information boards and parking and possibly the last water on the descent (**1hr 5min**, 1125m).

Cross the col and follow an undulating traverse to reach a minor road (**2hr 5min**, 935m). Turn left and

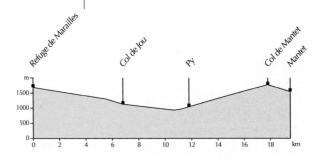

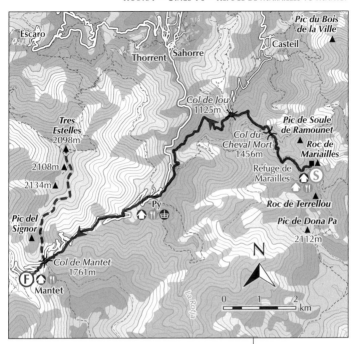

pass a (possibly dry) water point at La Farga. Join the 'main' road, then follow a track which shortcuts switchbacks in the road to arrive at the centre of **Py** (**2hr 25min**, N42°29.740 E002°21.051) with water point, gîte d'étape (no meals) and the Auberge de Py (with chambres d'hôtes accommodation, bar-restaurant and small épicerie).

Continue up the road, pass a picnic site and information boards and, about 50 metres before the 'end of Py' road-sign, turn sharp right, then left, up a paved path to the edge of the village. Follow the well-marked path which shortcuts switchbacks in the road, eventually to arrive at the **Col de Mantet** (**4hr 25min**, 1761m, N42°28.886 E002°18.837) with a car park, information boards and some interesting sculptures. ▶

From the col you could climb Pic de Tres Estelles (2098m) to the north (up and down in 130min) or Cime de Pomarole (2456m) to the south.

Sculpture at Col de Mantet

Follow the path steeply down the other side of the col, again shortcutting switchbacks in the road. Pass the Gîte d'étape La Cavale and Auberge la Bouf'tic at the top of **Mantet** and continue down, past toilets, to Gîte d'étape La Girada and Gîte à la Ferme Cazenove and a water point (**4hr 50min**, 1538m, N42°28.613 E002°18.379).

FACILITIES FOR STAGE 10

Py

Gîte d'étape de Py, accommodation but not meals: tel (33) 0468 05 66 28 or (33) 0612 04 84 91 http://bivouac.free.fr

Auberge de Py, chambres d'hôtes: tel (33) 0434 52 02 84

Mantet

Gîte d'étape la Girada: tel (33) 0468 05 68 69 or (33) 0630 15 66 51 www.lagirada.com

Gîte à la Ferme Cazenove, chambres d'hôtes: tel (33) 0468 05 60 99 www.gitecazenovemantet.fr

Auberge la Bouf'tic, chambres d'hôtes with bar-restaurant: tel (33) 0468 80 80 80 http://aubergelabouftic.wix.com/auberge-mantet

Gîte d'étape la Cavale, gîte d'étape and chambres d'hôtes accommodation with riding centre: tel (33) 0468 05 57 59 http://la-cavale.fr

STAGE 11

Mantet to
Refuge du Ras de la Carança

Start	Mantet
Distance	13km
Total ascent	900m
Total descent	600m
Time	4hr 30min
High points	ENE ridge of Pic de la Serre Gallinière (2334m)

This is a short stage, climbing up a classic alpine valley and over the Coll del Pal. Hikers who are just walking the eight-stage tour of Canigou will start this stage then shortcut over the Porteille de Mantet to the Refuge Ull de Ter in Spain.

From **Mantet** continue down to the main stream, Rivière de Ressec (1475m), and cross it. If the water level is high use a bridge downstream. Keep straight on then cross the Rivière d'Alemany and follow the path well above the stream to a signed junction (**1hr 40min**, 1960m, N42°27.499 E002°16.929).

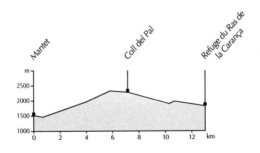

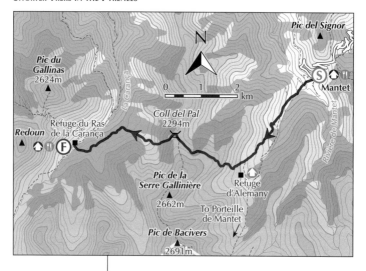

Looking back at Col de Mantet over Mantet

If you fork left, in a couple of minutes you'll come to the **Refuge d'Alemany**, a well-maintained bothy with water point and toilet. This is also the link to

the Refuge Ull de Ter in Spain, over the Porteille de Mantet, for those who are doing the eight-stage tour of Canigou.

Fork right along the GR10 for the full route and climb to the ENE ridge of Pic de la Serre Gallinière (**2hr 40min**, 2334m, N42°27.548 E002°15.508). ▶ Keep straight on and contour to **Coll del Pal** (**3hr**, 2294m, N42°27.918 E002°15.508). Just before the col you pass a trickling stream from a spring higher up the hill (dry September 2016).

The proliferation of paths/animal tracks on the descent means care is needed following the waymarks. Initially descend left and veer right after passing through a gate. As you near the bottom of the hill (**3hr 50min**, 1900m) veer left and climb gently. Eventually (1980m) veer right to cross a stream and follow the GR10 down to a bridge over the Rivière de la Caranza. Cross the stream and veer right to the **Refuge du Ras de la Caranza**, with aire de bivouac (**4hr 30min**, 1830m, N42°27.862 E002°13.432).

It would be easy to climb this peak (2563m), or even Pic de la Dona (2702m) on the border ridge.

FACILITIES FOR STAGE 11

Refuge du Ras de la Caranza: tel (33) 0988 67 73 81 www.refugedelacaranca.com

STAGE 12
Refuge du Ras de la Caranza to Eyne

Start	Refuge du Ras de la Caranza
Distance	26km
Total ascent	1100m
Total descent	1300m
Time	7hr 25min
High points	Col Mitja (2367m)

This stage follows the GR10 until Planès, then the GR36 to Eyne, with red/
white waymarks. Depending on the start/finish point of your trek and your
transport arrangements, there is a case for ending this long stage at the
impressive Gîte d'étape L'Orri de Planès and adding an extra stage for the
short walk to Eyne.

Follow the track that starts from the north side of the
Refuge du Ras de la Carança and climb. Either follow
the track all the way to the col (recommended) or follow

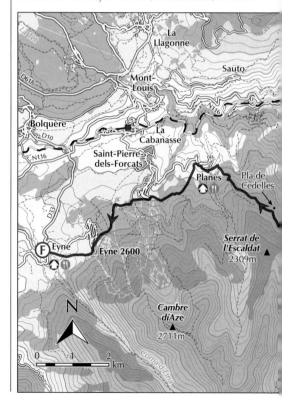

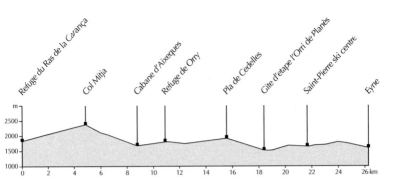

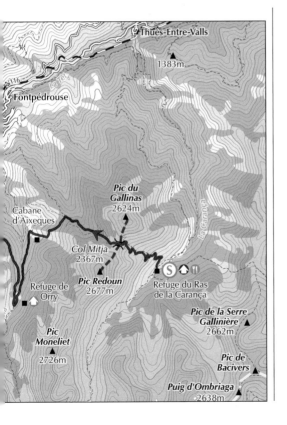

263

Pic Redoun from Pic de Gallinas

Pic de Gallinas (2624m) to the northeast and Pic Redoun (2677m) to the southwest both provide worthwhile climbs (both take about 75min up and down).

the steeper GR10 which shortcuts the switchbacks in the track to reach the **Col Mitja** (**1hr 45min** (by track), 2367m, N42°28.319 E002°12.758). ◀

The initial descent from the col isn't clearly way-marked, but the GR10 again shortcuts switchbacks in the track. Pass a reliable spring-fed pipe (**2hr 5min**, 2110m) and contour to the grassy Collets d'Aval with a rough shepherds' hut. Again, shortcut the track and soon reach good sheltered campsites, then follow the track for a short distance before going straight on at a switchback and descending a steep path through rough terrain to the tiny **Cabane d'Aixeques** (**2hr 55min**, 1688m), only suitable for an emergency bivouac.

Follow the track left, then turn left and follow it upstream, ignoring side-turns, to reach the **Refuge de Orry** (**3hr 30min**, 1810m, N42°27.633 E002°10.543) with water point. This herdsman's hut has a room available as a bothy to hikers.

Continue a short distance upstream, cross a bridge over **La Ribérola**, by a well-preserved *orri*, and follow the vague path downstream. After a time, the path starts edging away from the stream then it eventually (**3hr 55min**, 1750m) starts rising for an undulating traverse. Cross a small stream shortly before a col, **Pla de Cedelles** (**4hr 50min**, 1911m, N42°28.772 E002°09.696) with excellent camping.

Follow well-waymarked paths, tracks and eventually roads down to the Gîte d'étape L'Orri de Planès at the top of **Planès** (**5hr 30min**, 1530m, N42°29.462 E002°08.310).

Continue down through Planès, passing several water points. Turn left and then left again across a bridge and follow the road to a signpost immediately after the Chambres d'hôte Le Malaza. The route leaves the GR10 here; turn left along the well-waymarked GR36, signed to Eyne (**5hr 35min**). Soon fork right along a path that climbs before contouring and then descending a little to cross a stream (**6hr 10min**) and reaching the buildings at the top of the Saint-Pierre ski centre (**6hr 15min**, 1650m). Fork left and then right by some communication masts and turn left at a rough parking area (**6hr 35min**), then climb to a smaller communication mast (**6hr 55min**).

Pass through the top car park at **Eyne 2600** ski resort, where it is possible some facilities could be open in July/ August. At the end of the resort, turn left and right and follow a track downhill to the Gîte Cal-Pai in **Eyne** (**7hr 25min**, 1595m, N42°28.408 E002°04.967).

FACILITIES FOR STAGE 12

Planès

Gîte d'étape l'Orri de Planès, gîte d'étape and chambres d'hôtes accommodation with full meals service, picnic lunches, camping area and swimming pool: tel (33) 0468 04 29 47 or (33) 0622 32 25 32 www.orrideplanes.com

Chambres d'hôtes Malaza: tel (33) 0468 04 20 99

Eyne

See Stage 1

APPENDIX A
Route summary tables

Stage no	Stage title	Distance	Ascent	Descent	Time	Page
Route 1						
Stage 1	St-Jean-Pied-de-Port – Saint-Étienne-de-Baïgorry	20km	900m	900m	5hr 15min	36
Stage 2	Saint-Étienne-de-Baïgorry – Bidarray	19km	1400m	1400m	6hr 45min	40
Stage 3	Bidarray – Ainhoa	26km	900m	900m	6hr 30min	44
Stage 4	Ainhoa – Sare	13km	200m	200m	2hr 55min	50
Stage 5	Sare – Bera	17km	900m	900m	4hr 50min	53
Stage 6	Bera – Elizondo	33km	1200m	1000m	8hr 20min	57
Stage 7	Elizondo – Aldudes	17km	900m	600m	4hr 45min	63
Stage 8	Aldudes – Burguete	21km	1100m	700m	6hr 25min	67
Stage 9	Burguete – St Jean Pied-de-Port	28km	600m	1300m	6hr 15min	72
		194km	**8100m**	**8100m**	**52hr**	
Route 2						
Stage 1	Etsaut – Camping du Lauzart (Lescun)	17km	1100m	900m	4hr 50min	80
Stage 2	Camping du Lauzart (Lescun) – Refugio de Linza	20km	1300m	800m	6hr 5min	84
Stage 3	Refugio de Linza – Refugio de Gabardito	26km	1600m	1600m	8hr 20min	87
Stage 4	Refugio de Gabardito – Refugio de Lizara	11km	700m	500m	3hr 5min	91

Stage no	Stage title	Distance	Ascent	Descent	Time	Page
Stage 5	Refugio de Lizara – Col du Somport	20km	900m	800m	6hr 10min	95
Stage 6	Col du Somport – Refuge de Pombie	16km	1300m	900m	5hr 40min	98
Stage 7	Refuge de Pombie – Refuge d'Ayous	14km	700m	800m	3hr 35min	102
Stage 8	Refuge d'Ayous – Etsaut	17km	300m	1600m	3hr 55min	105
		141km	**7900m**	**7900m**	**42hr**	

Route 3

Stage no	Stage title	Distance	Ascent	Descent	Time	Page
Stage 1	Cauterets – Refuge des Oulettes de Gaube	21km	1400m	200m	6hr 35min	111
Stage 2	Refuge des Oulettes de Gaube – Refuge des Granges de Holle	22km	800m	1400m	6hr 50min	116
Stage 3	Refuge des Granges de Holle – Refuge des Éspuguettes	10km	700m	200m	2hr 55min	121
Stage 4	Refuge des Éspuguettes – Refugio de Pineta	21km	900m	1700m	7hr 35min	124
Stage 5	Refugio de Pineta – Refugio de Góriz	19km	1900m	1000m	7hr 55min	128
Stage 6	Refugio de Góriz – Refuge de la Brèche de Roland	9km	800m	400m	3hr 30min	132
Stage 7	Refuge de la Brèche de Roland – Refugio de Bujaruelo	10km	50m	1300m	3hr	135
Stage 8	Refugio de Bujaruelo – Baños de Panticosa	24km	1300m	1000m	7hr 40min	137
Stage 9	Baños de Panticosa – Refugio de Respomuso	17km	1300m	700m	6hr 40min	141
Stage 10	Refugio de Respomuso – Refuge Wallon	12km	600m	1000m	4hr 25min	144
Stage 11	Refuge Wallon – Cauterets	21km	800m	1700m	6hr 45min	147
		186km	**10,600m**	**10,600m**	**64hr**	

Stage no	Stage title	Distance	Ascent	Descent	Time	Page
Route 4						
Stage 1	Barèges – Artigues	20km	1200m	1200m	5hr 30min	153
Stage 2	Artigues – Refuge de Campana de Cloutou	10km	1100m	100m	3hr 50min	158
Stage 3	Refuge de Campana de Cloutou – Lac d'Orédon	16km	800m	1200m	5hr 10min	161
Stage 4	Lac d'Orédon – Barèges	24km	800m	1400m	6hr 10min	165
		70km	**3900m**	**3900m**	**21hr**	
Route 5						
Stage 1	Refugi dera Restanca – Refugi Joan Ventosa i Calvell	11km	600m	400m	3hr 50min	173
Stage 2	Refugi Joan Ventosa i Calvell – Refugi d'Estany Llong	14km	800m	1000m	5hr 30min	176
Stage 3	Refugi d'Estany Llong – Refugi de la Colomina	14km	800m	400m	4hr 50min	179
Stage 4	Refugi de la Colomina – Refugi JM Blanc	9km	400m	500m	3hr 30min	182
Stage 5	Refugi JM Blanc – Refugi Sant Maurici Ernest Mallafré	12km	500m	900m	3hr 35min	185
Stage 6	Refugi Sant Maurici Ernest Mallafré – Refugi de Saboredo	12km	700m	300m	4hr 10min	189
Stage 7	Refugi de Saboredo– Refugi dera Restanca	17km	900m	1200m	6hr 15min	192
		89km	**4700m**	**4700m**	**32hr**	

Stage no	Stage title	Distance	Ascent	Descent	Time	Page
Route 6						
Stage 1	Ax-les-Thermes – Orlu	7km	200m	50m	1hr 35min	198
Stage 2	Orlu – Refuge d'en Beys	22km	1600m	500m	8hr 25min	201
Stage 3	Refuge d'en Beys – Refuge de Camporells	13km	900m	600m	4hr 50min	204
Stage 4	Refuge de Camporells – Refuge des Bouillouses	13km	400m	600m	3hr 20min	208
Stage 5	Refuge des Bouillouses – Refuge des Bésines	19km	800m	700m	6hr 20min	210
Stage 6	Refuge des Bésines – Auberge du Nabre (Mérens-les-Vals)	11km	300m	1200m	3hr 30min	215
Stage 7	Auberge du Nabre – Refuge de Rulhe	16km	1600m	600m	6hr 15min	217
Stage 8	Refuge de Rulhe – Ax-les-Thermes	24km	400m	1900m	6hr 40min	220
		125km	**6500m**	**6500m**	**41hr**	
Route 7						
Stage 1	Eyne – Núria	17km	1100m	700m	5hr	228
Stage 2	Traverse of Puigmal from Núria	19km	1300m	1300m	5hr 50min	232
Stage 3	Núria – Refugi de Ull de Ter (via Refugi de Coma de Vaca)	19km	900m	700m	5hr 35min	234
Stage 4	Refugi de Ull de Ter – Chalet de las Conques	17km	400m	1100m	4hr 35min	238
Stage 5	Chalet de las Conques – Refuge de Saint-Guillem	24km	800m	1100m	6hr 30min	241
Stage 6	Refuge de Saint-Guillem – Refuge de Batère	22km	1200m	1000m	6hr 10min	245
Stage 7	Refuge de Batère – Refuge des Cortalets	18km	1100m	400m	5hr	248

Stage no	Stage title	Distance	Ascent	Descent	Time	Page
Stage 8	Traverse of Canigou	9km	800m	800m	3hr 30min	251
Stage 9	Refuge des Cortalets – Refuge de Marailles	20km	500m	1000m	5hr 25min	253
Stage 10	Refuge de Marailles – Mantet	20km	900m	1100m	4hr 50min	256
Stage 11	Mantet – Refuge du Ras de la Carança	13km	900m	600m	4hr 30min	259
Stage 12	Refuge du Ras de la Carança – Eyne	26km	1100m	1300m	7hr 25min	261
		224km	**11,000m**	**11,000m**	**65hr**	

APPENDIX B
Sources of information

Maps
In 2017 Editorial Alpina published an excellent 1:50,000 map for the GR11 to add to their excellent range of maps and guides to the Pyrenees: www.editorialalpina.com

IGN is France's equivalent of the UK's Ordnance Survey and it provides full coverage of the French Pyrenees and the most popular areas of the Spanish Pyrenees at 1:50,000: www.ign.fr

FFRandonnée cover the French Pyrenees in four Topoguides with 1:50,000 maps giving full coverage of the GR10 and many shorter treks: www.ffrandonnee.fr

Maps are available from many sources including:

Maps Worldwide Ltd: www.mapsworldwide.com

The Map Shop: www.themapshop.co.uk

Edward Stanford Ltd: www.stanfords.co.uk

Cordee Ltd: www.cordee.co.uk

Mountain refuges
Information and booking for albergues, manned and unmanned refuges in Aragón: www.fam.es and www.alberguesyrefugiosdearagon.com

Information and booking for refuges in Catalonia: www.feec.cat, tel (34) 934 120 777

For tourist information and information on refuges in Andorra: https://visitandorra.com/en

The French Alpine Club site gives up-to date information on mountain refuges in France: www.ffcam.fr

Details on gîtes d'étape and refuges on the GR10: http://peyo.free.fr/refuges.htm

Weather forecasts
www.mountain-forecast.com

French weather forecasts: www.meteofrance.com

Spanish weather forecasts: www.spainweather.es

Severe weather warnings for Europe: www.meteoalarm.eu

Historical and current snow depths at a number of French Pyrenees ski resorts which may help planning if you are contemplating an early season hike: www.onthesnow.co.uk

Telephone codes
Europe-wide emergency telephone number: 112

International telephone codes:

UK: 44 (dial 0044 from France or Spain)

France: 33 (dial 0033 from UK)

Spain: 34 (dial 0034 from UK)

Andorra: 376 (dial 00376 from UK)

Travel information
P&O car ferries: www.poferries.com

Brittany Ferries: www.brittany-ferries.co.uk

National Express coaches: www.nationalexpress.com

FlixBus coaches: www.flixbus.co.uk

Eurotunnel: www.eurotunnel.com

Eurostar: www.eurostar.com

French rail network: www.sncf.com

Spanish rail network: www.renfe.com

Ryanair: www.ryanair.com

British Airways: www.britishairways.com

Air France: www.airfrance.co.uk

Easyjet: www.easyjet.com

APPENDIX C

Bibliography

Other Cicerone guides to the Pyrenees (www.cicerone.co.uk):

The GR10 Trail by Brian Johnson (2016)

The GR11 Trail by Brian Johnson (2018)

The Pyrenean Haute Route by Tom Martens (2019)

Walks and Climbs in the Pyrenees by Kev Reynolds (2017)

The Mountains of Andorra by Alf Robertson and Jane Meadowcroft (2005)

The Pyrenees by Kev Reynolds (2010)

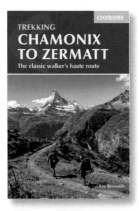
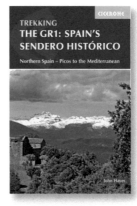

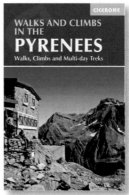

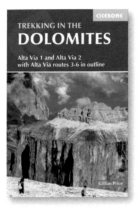
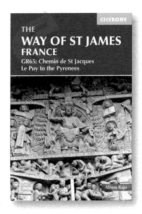
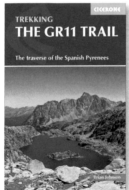

LISTING OF CICERONE GUIDES

SCOTLAND

Backpacker's Britain:
  Northern Scotland
Ben Nevis and Glen Coe
Cycling in the Hebrides
Great Mountain Days in Scotland
Mountain Biking in Southern and
  Central Scotland
Mountain Biking in West and
  North West Scotland
Not the West Highland Way
Scotland
Scotland's Best Small Mountains
Scotland's Mountain Ridges
Scrambles in Lochaber
The Ayrshire and Arran Coastal
  Paths
The Border Country
The Borders Abbeys Way
The Cape Wrath Trail
The Great Glen Way
The Great Glen Way Map Booklet
The Hebridean Way
The Hebrides
The Isle of Mull
The Isle of Skye
The Skye Trail
The Southern Upland Way
The Speyside Way
The Speyside Way Map Booklet
The West Highland Way
Walking Highland Perthshire
Walking in Scotland's Far North
Walking in the Angus Glens
Walking in the Cairngorms
Walking in the Ochils, Campsie
  Fells and Lomond Hills
Walking in the Pentland Hills
Walking in the Southern Uplands
Walking in Torridon
Walking Loch Lomond and the
  Trossachs
Walking on Arran
Walking on Harris and Lewis
Walking on Rum and the Small
  Isles
Walking on the Orkney and
  Shetland Isles
Walking on Uist and Barra
Walking the Corbetts Vol 1 South
  of the Great Glen
Walking the Corbetts Vol 2 North
  of the Great Glen
Walking the Munros
  Vol 1 – Southern, Central and
  Western Highlands
Walking the Munros
  Vol 2 – Northern Highlands
  and the Cairngorms

West Highland Way Map Booklet
Winter Climbs Ben Nevis and
  Glen Coe
Winter Climbs in the Cairngorms

NORTHERN ENGLAND TRAILS

Hadrian's Wall Path
Hadrian's Wall Path Map Booklet
Pennine Way Map Booklet
The Coast to Coast Map Booklet
The Coast to Coast Walk
The Dales Way
The Dales Way Map Booklet
The Pennine Way

LAKE DISTRICT

Cycling in the Lake District
Great Mountain Days in the Lake
  District
Lake District Winter Climbs
Lake District: High Level and
  Fell Walks
Lake District: Low Level and
  Lake Walks
Mountain Biking in the Lake
  District
Outdoor Adventures with
  Children – Lake District
Scrambles in the Lake District
  – North
Scrambles in the Lake District
  – South
Short Walks in Lakeland
  Book 1: South Lakeland
Short Walks in Lakeland
  Book 2: North Lakeland
Short Walks in Lakeland
  Book 3: West Lakeland
The Cumbria Way
Tour of the Lake District
Trail and Fell Running in the Lake
  District

NORTH WEST ENGLAND
AND THE ISLE OF MAN

Cycling the Pennine Bridleway
Cycling the Way of the Roses
Isle of Man Coastal Path
The Lancashire Cycleway
The Lune Valley and Howgills
The Ribble Way
Walking in Cumbria's Eden Valley
Walking in Lancashire
Walking in the Forest of Bowland
  and Pendle
Walking on the Isle of Man
Walking on the West Pennine
  Moors
Walks in Ribble Country
Walks in Silverdale and Arnside

NORTH EAST ENGLAND,
YORKSHIRE DALES
AND PENNINES

Cycling in the Yorkshire Dales
Great Mountain Days in the
  Pennines
Mountain Biking in the Yorkshire
  Dales
South Pennine Walks
St Oswald's Way and
  St Cuthbert's Way
The Cleveland Way and the
  Yorkshire Wolds Way
The Cleveland Way Map Booklet
The North York Moors
The Reivers Way
The Teesdale Way
Trail and Fell Running in the
  Yorkshire Dales
Walking in County Durham
Walking in Northumberland
Walking in the North Pennines
Walking in the Yorkshire Dales:
  North and East
Walking in the Yorkshire Dales:
  South and West
Walks in Dales Country
Walks in the Yorkshire Dales

WALES AND WELSH BORDERS

Cycling Lôn Las Cymru
Glyndwr's Way
Great Mountain Days in
  Snowdonia
Hillwalking in Shropshire
Hillwalking in Wales – Vol 1
Hillwalking in Wales – Vol 2
Mountain Walking in Snowdonia
Offa's Dyke Map Booklet
Offa's Dyke Path
Ridges of Snowdonia
Scrambles in Snowdonia
The Ascent of Snowdon
The Ceredigion and Snowdonia
  Coast Paths
The Pembrokeshire Coast Path
Pembrokeshire Coast Path Map
  Booklet
The Severn Way
The Snowdonia Way
The Wales Coast Path
The Wye Valley Walk
Walking in Carmarthenshire
Walking in Pembrokeshire
Walking in the Forest of Dean
Walking in the South Wales
  Valleys
Walking in the Wye Valley
Walking on the Brecon Beacons
Walking on the Gower